ENGLISH RECUSANT LITERATURE
1558–1640

Selected and Edited by
D. M. ROGERS

Volume 144

FRANCOIS VERON
M. Le Hucher . . . Compelled to Fly
[1616]

LUKE WADDING
The History of . . . S. Clare
1635

FRANCOIS VERON

M. Le Hucher . . . Compelled to Fly
[1616]

The Scolar Press
1973

ISBN 0 85417 952 6

Published and Printed in Great Britain by
The Scolar Press Limited, 20 Main Street,
Menston, Yorkshire, England

NOTE

The following works are reproduced (original size), with permission:

1) Francois Veron, *M. Le Hucher . . . compelled to fly*, [1616], from a copy in the library of Sion College, by permission of the Librarian.

References: Allison and Rogers 843; STC 15400.

2) Luke Wadding, *The history of . . . S. Clare*, 1635, from a copy in the library of Stonyhurst College, by permission of the Rector.

References: Allison and Rogers 869; STC 24924.

M. LE HVCHER

MINISTER

OF AMYENS IN

FRANCE COMPELLED
to fly from the pure word of Holy
write; ſtrucke dumme; and made
to runne away.

*Vppon the ſubiect of the B. Sacrament
of the Altar.*

By F. FRANCIS VERON of the
Society of IESVS, encountring
him with the Bible of
Geneua only.

In the preſence of the Duke de Longueuille.

VVith a briefe and eaſie meanes, by which
each Catholicke may, in like manner, put
to flight any Miniſter or Sectarie.

*Sent from Sieur de la Tour one of the ſayd
Dukes Gentlemen, to Sieur de Rotois,
Gentleman of the Kings game.*

Printed
With Licence of Superiours.

Explication of the Title.

This Conference was held three seuerall times. In the first the Father of the Society; compelled the Mini-fter to abandone the pure word of the holie fcripture ; In the 2. he putt him to filence ; In the 3. he made him runne away.

Testimony of the said conference.

It is figned by the Father of the Society; by the Duke of Longueuil-les Gentlemen who accompanying theyr Lord were prefent therat ; and in parte by the Minifter, which refufed to fubcribe to that, which putt him moft to confufion. The fubcriptions follow in theyr proper place.

To the Reader.

WO things there are (good
Reader) wich made me (desirous of thy eternall good)
to turne for thy vse this lit-
tle treatise into our language. The one the
breuity and pleasure it yealdeth, the other
the easines and perspicuity, with which it
confuteth, it instructeth. The first suteth
well to that lazy humour, which heresy
hath brought into our country , wherby
men haue little gust to read ought, that
concernes their soules, and scarse ought of
that, vnles it be well seasoned with extraordinary delight. The other (supposing thy
capacity, and affection to truth, which if
affection misleade me not, is equall to that
of most Nations, and by heresy I hope not
maliciously peruerted, or at least not pur-
uersly obstinate therin) makes me presume
thou wilt easily see, and quickly leaue that

A 2   blind

blind mans maze, of the falsly pure pre-
tended word, wherin thou hast beene long
ledde round. Both of them, by Gods aßi-
stance, promiße vnto me no little fruite of
this small worke, which is that I hartely
desyre for thy soules good, and Gods grea-
ter glory. Farewell.

Thy welwiller in
IESVS CHRIST.
D. V.

A LETTER OF
Mr. DE LA TOVR

GENTLEMAN TO THE
DVKE OF LONGVEVILLE.

VVritten vnto Mr. de Rotois Gen-
tleman of the Kings game.

Y R the ardent zeale I
know you haue of the
good and glory of our
Religion, makes me suppose you wil receaue a singular content in the relation of a priuate conference, had of late in the presence of my Lord the Duke of Longueuille and his followers, of the Marques de Boniuet, of the Lady de Bourcq & diuers others aswell Catholiks as Sectaries, between Father

A 3   Fran-

Francis Veron of the Society of IE-
svs, preacher for this present in the
great Church of this Citty, & M. le
Hucher Minister of the Caluinists in
the same place, touching that point
of our Faith, of the body of the sóne
of God in the Sacrament of the Altar. The said Father agreeing to deale
with that Minister by the Bible of
Geneua only, and the Confession of
faith of the reformed. This conference hath had three sessions, at the
first I was not present, not being ad-
uertised of the same. Notwithstanding at the beginning of the second,
the actes of the former session were
read, alowed & auowed by both par-
ties as authenticall. Wherfore I will
make recitall of that which passed in
the sight of my Lord, & vs that were
attending on him, besides a great
multitude of diuerse of the one, and
the other Religion. The said Father
on the morrow after the last conference which was Sunday, made an
ample narration of the three passed
                                    mee-

meetings to aboue eight thowsand persones, assembled in the Church of our Lady to heare his sermon. The most heerof is signed as you will see after, wherfore no man can iustlie call in question a matter so cleerly testified.

Our Deuine atchieued three famous victories. For the Minister hauing promised conformably to the 31. and 5. articles of theyr Confession of their faith, to shew by the pure word of the Bible, that we erred in that beleefe we haue, that the body of our Lord is in the Eucharist, he was constrained in the first session and againe in the entrance vnto the second trial, to fly from his fortresse of the pure word, of force disclaiming from the pure scripture of Geneua: and withall aknowledged and cōfessed, that there was no expresse text in all the scripture, euen by the Geneua translation, which, (setting a side all illations, did condemne vs of errour. But (quoth the Minister) by

A 4   ne-

neceſſary conſequence out of the pure worde of God I will make it cleare that you do erre.

The night comming on made our combatant ceaſe the purſuite, & not driue him farther, who already ſheltred himſelf within the ruinous edifice of a Conſequence. The Father told me, that it was not of ſmall importāce, to make the Sectaries cleatly ſee & confeſſe, that they haue not for themſelues the pure ſcripture, but only certain conſequences, for (quoth he) the cauſe that makes ſo many to beginne, and continue in their reuolt from Gods Church, is for that they perſuade themſelues, that they haue on their ſides the pure word of God; for ſo ſaith the 5. article of their Confeſſion, that they admitt nothing for the rule of faith, but the pure word: & they do veryly ſuppoſe that that Confeſſion conteineth nothing, but that which is in the pure worde. After the approbation of that paſſed before, the Mini-

Minister at the second session was
admitted to deduce his necessary
consequence, by which he would
demostrate how farre we wandred
from the truth. He first fetched long
vagaries round about, afterward the
Father so dexterously put him beside
all his proofes, & in briefe brought
him to such pangues, that for the finall proposition he had nothing to
say against the Father, but, ô you deny to much; after which he became
alltogeather speechles, as I wil more
largely declare her after. Certes you
would haue been extraordinarily re-
created to behold, how he that ere-
while made profession to proue by
the pure word of God that we were
Idolaters, in lieu of the pure word,
had not a word to help himself, saue
this only, that the Iesuite denied to
much, wee I am sure had good sport
therin. Ours which had thus chased
the Minister, still put him to these pa-
gues for a long time still vrging him
thus. M. Minister prooue your con-

sequence. Neither did he omitt to signifie plainly and alowde to the whole assemblie, to what exigents the poore Minister was brought to, who sustained the Confession of the faith of the reformed Religion, and bragged to discouer by the pure word our errours. Had not the quality of the Ministers cause been such as it was, I should haue had compassion to haue seen him in that plight, and so oppressed. He desired they would giue him that night for respite, and to thinke vppon it; but the Father denied him; he alleaged he was suddainly surprised, the other replied that he had had all the night, and morning before for his proofe of that consequence. It was not neede to take pitty of the Minister, for his fellow Sectaries had sufficient comiseration of him; all of them round about me beganne to change coulour, the Elders and Superintendents stood as it were astonished, & cofounded. You may coniecture easily
fily

fily whether we were ioyfull thereat
or no. Alas (faid one) the poore Minifter wants a Chirurgian to open
him a vayne. This victory was more
notorious by this which followeth.
The conquerour exacted of the van-
quisshed to fubfcribe to the Acts of
this conference, according to the accord made between them. A lamen-
table cafe! that the ouercome muft
fubfcribe to the actes of his owne
condemnation. He refufed to performe his promiffe. The Father after many inftant vrgings of him in
vaine, turned towards my Lord, and
demaunded iuftice; that the Minifter figne according as he had pro-
mifed. The Minifter defired fauour,
befeeching him often that he would
not cómaund him to fubfcribe, after
many prayers adding thefe wordes.
I know how much it ftands me
vppon not to figne, for if I do fo, all
will be publifhed: and the Churches
(you vnderftand his meaning at leaft
his lamenting voice difcouered his
                              inten-

intention) the poore congregations
(he should say) of the pure reformation will be scandalized therat.
The Father hauing before desired
one of ours to shutt the doore, least
the Minister should runne away, bid
him consult with his Elders, and
Superintendents, whether it were
expedient to signe the actes or no :
for which cause drawing them apart
it was resolued that he should not
signe them. I will send you shortly more at large this debate, which
lasted three quarters of an howre.
In fine, with the consent of the Father, they graunted him this fauour
that he should not subscribe, but
with these two conditions : the first
that he should subscribe the morrow after; the second that he should
continew the dispute. By this refu-
fall to subscribe vnto the Actes, it is
apparent how notable the victorie
was on our parte.

In the third encounter our Champion gott a third victory, but in an
other

other kind; will you knowe what?
The Miniſter ſhamefully rann away.
He was not willing to be laid againe
a gaſping as before, and therfore
thought it better not to inter into
the liſtes, as I will declare afterward.
It was giuen out that the Superin-
tendentes had expreſlie forbidd him
to venture himſelfe with him, who
before had vſed him ſo vnmerciful-
ly, for they well ſaw the confuſion
like to follow therof, to the great
detriment of their Churches.

Your Religious minde makes me
preſume you take great delight in
this chace; I will therfore giue you
the whole narration. But yett before hand I wil shew you a new máner of hunting which, though you
be moſt skilfuil in that ſport, is perchance vnknowne vnto you. The
faſhion is ſpeedy, with little paines,
and moſt effectuall, by which pra-
ctiſe our Huntſman hath ſo happily
ſeazed on his pray: and by the ſame I
aſſure my ſelf, that euen we whoſe
pro-

profession is to be better at our weapon then our penne, may chace out of breath any Minister soeuer, and make any Sectarie see how grosslie he is abused. This I haue compiled as a thing I knowe to be true, and wherof I meane to serue my self on all occasions. In this Conference I haue had experience of this practise, for therein was held no other methode; & to satisfy your desire, who I knowe are curious to learne this new manner of hunting, you may read this which followeth, the like wherof was sent vnto the Minister as a letter of defiance. Read it seriously. To me it seemes most efficacious and as easy. Wee shall all prooue hunters of these black beastes, the Ministers I meane of the pretended Religion. I would to God we could so chace away not their persons, but their errours, that we could purge all France thereof. This I now send you laid downe at large, you shall shortly haue the particulars of the confe-

rence

rence aboue mentioned, in which
you will see it practised.

A BREEFE AND EASIE
meanes by vvhich each one though
ignorant of deuinity, may by the
sole Bible either of Geneua, or any
other, shevv apperently to any Mi-
nister hovv farre he is deceaued,
andto each Caluinist, hovv in all
and euery point of the pretended
reformation he is abused.

NCOVNTRING a
Minister or anie o-
ther Caluinist, you
shall proceed in this
manner.

You haue in the 31. article of the
Cófession of your faith these words.
In our dayes, in wbich the estate of the
Church was dissolued, God hath raised men
after an extraordinar. manner to repaire

of

of new the Church which was ruinated
and desolate. Thus, you say, your Religion comes to reforme our errours.

In the 5. article are these words.
*The word which is contayned in these
bookes* (he spake of the bookes of Holy Scripture) *is the rule of all truth, containing all that is necessary for the seruice
of God, and our saluation; Neither is it
lawfull for men, no nor for Angells, to
adde, diminish, or change. VVhence it followeth that neither Antiquitie, nor Customes, nor Multitude, nor humane Wisdome
nor Definitions, nor Inhibitions, nor Proclamations, nor Decrees, nor Councels, nor
Reuelations, nor Miracles may be opposed
to the said holy Scriptures, but on the contrarie all thinges ar to be examined, ruled,
and reformed by them.* These are the
wordes of this article.

So that in the one and the other
article mētioned togeather, you say
that you, or your Religion, or your
Ministers (take your choise) are raised and sent from God, to illuminate
vs with the light of truth, & to shew

vs

vs our errours and that by the sole, and pure word of God contained in the holy Scripture.

1. First I might examine the conditions of these Reformers you thrust vpon vs. And vntill you shew me your letter patents and commission, I may iustly refuse to submitt my selfto be reformed by you. What body politicque will allow the title of Reformour of their Lawes, and Customes (according to which they haue hitherto proceeded in their gouernment) in one who should say he was sent from the King for that purpose, but had no Commission to shew for the same? Notwithstanding in curtesy I do freely admitt you to the dignity and title of a Reformer, & am content to be instructed by you in the truth, and to be reformed in whatsoeuer I do erre. I would know of you.

2. According to what rules, by what line doth it please you to straighten me, to shew my errours, and

and illuminate me with the truth of
the Gospell? You make me answeare
in the 5. article aboue cited, that you
will do all this according to the pure
word of God, sett downe in Holie
writt, laying aside, *All Antiquity, Customes, Multitude, humane VVisdome,
Definitions, Inhibitions, Proclamations,
Lawes, Councels, Reuelations, Miracles*. I
could refuse this fashion of reforming. For why should I not, togeather with the Scripture, help my self
with all other rules to discerne the
truth thereby? Especially since that
the Scripture no where saith, that it
self alone is the rule of all verity. It
seemes hard to me to renouce al Antiquity, Coūcels, Miracles, & all the
rest before sett downe. Neuertheles
to ioyne with you in Conference, I
am content of my owne accord to
graunt you the title of Reformer by
the pure written word, & am ready
to renounce al those rules specified,
prouided allwaies that you keepe
your promise, to witt that you shew
me

me my errours, by the pure Scripture.

3.   There are diuers tranflations
of the Scriptures; by which, I pray
you, will you pleafe to reforme me?
Perchance you intēd by that of Geneua. I might iuftly refufe to be reformed by that Bible; being it is fo
curtalled in diuers places, corrupted,
and changed: Yet to haue your reformation I wil do you this third fauour. I am content to open my eyes
and follow your Religion, if you
shew my by the pure word contained in the Geneua verfion, both the
truth of the faith you Euangelize, &
allfo my errours. I haue donne you
three great fauours. 1. to graunt you
the title of a Reformer. 2. to be a Reformer by the pure word. The third
to make this triall by the pure word
of the Geneua verfion. But looke
you bring me nothing els but the
pure word; for if in fteede of it you
shift me of with your interpretations, you forfake the Confeffion of
                          your

your faith, & breake the couenants made betweene vs. For I am not so vnaduised to renounce all Antiquity, Councells, Miracles and the rest, for your interpretations and opinions.

Agreeably to this, to your owne promise, & that which is sett downe in your 5. article, I demaund two things at your hands. First that you shew me by the pure word the truth of all those articles which you will haue me to beleeue: which I am ready to do, if I see them in the Bible euen of Geneua. Secondly that by the same pure word you shew me my errours. Both of these I demand, for both of these you professe to do when as you say, that *the Scripture is the rule of all truth*, and you acknowledge no other. For put the case I should erre in my faith, I would be loth to leaue that, to follow a worse. No wise man, I take it, though his horse haue but one eye wil make exchāge for another that is blind; I desire

sire therfore to see by the pure word the truth of yours. Which you cánot refuse to do, for you are sent to illu-minate vs, & shew vs the truth. To be plaine therfore, my first demaund is, that you shew me by the pure word the Articles of your Confes-sió, by which I must be illuminated, and made to knowe the right way.

In the 36. and 37. article you say that *we receaue by faith*, or, to vse your ordinary termes, *by the mouth of faith the body of our Lord.* Shew me this in the pure word, & that the supper is the figure of his body. Through all the Geneua Bible I find not so much as mention made of the mouth of faith, neither do I finde any talke of a figure in those places, where it speakes of the supper. Shew me but this, & I will straight beleeue it and abiure my former Religion. This if you do not, I must needs hold you, as you ar, for impostours.

In the 11. article it is said. *Origi-nall sinne doth continually remaine after*

Bap-

Baptisme in asmuch as it is a fault, howbeit the children of God are freed from the codemnation due for the same, he through his gracious goodnes not imputing it vnto them Shew me this in the pure word of Geneua.

In the 24. article. *Iesus Christ is giuen vs for our sole Aduocate,* The strife between vs is about that worde *Sole,* shew me that in the Geneua Bible.

In the 20. article. We beleeue *we are made partakers of that iustice (* to witt of Christians *) by faith alone.* All the controuersie lyeth in that word *alone,* and whether workes donne in the faith of Christ be necessary; shew me that worde *alone* in these places, where mention is made of workes donne in the faith of IESVS CHRIST, and not in these places, where the Iudaicall workes of the law are excluded from Christian iustification, for of these only do we dispute. I haue turned the Bible for the places cited in the margent for these articles, but cannot find any of these articles

ticles in the pure word.

Hauing quitt your hands well, in shewing me the truth of that which you defire I should beleeue, shew me as well that other thing I demaunde, to witt the errours of thofe articles which I now beleeue.

The articles of my faith are for example (to omitt that point of the B. Sacrement allready fpoken of) *That there is a Purgatory, Interceſſion of Saints, Auricular Confeſſion, and the like. I acknowledge the sanctity of Pilgrimages, of Religious vowes*. Againſt which in your 24. article you fay. *Interceſſion of Saints is an abuſe, Purgatorrie an illuſion and ſo of religious vowes, Pilgrimages and the like*. Shew me my errour in thefe points, & that out of the pure word. In your margent I find no text cited, which is a shrewd fufpició that you haue none. Perchance you wil aunfweare that it fufficeth for a proofe of errour in thefe points, that they are not found in the holy fcripture, becaufe nothing muſt be beleeued

but

but that which is in the scripture.
My reply to this is to know of you
whether this proposition. *That nothing must be beleeued which is not in the
holy scripture* be found in the pure
word of God or. If it be not, then
you M. Minister in propounding
this proposition to be beleeued of
me, do falsify your owne fayth, and
breake your promise; for you sayd
you wold not admitt any other rule
of truth but the scripture, which is
in effect, that you will bring forth
nothing but that which is in scripture, and now you thrust vpon me
this proposition, which is not there
to be found, & this as a fundamental
proposition vpon which ar builded
many others: but if this proposition
be in the pure word, shew it; but
take heede you bring nothing, but
the pure word.

When by the pure word you shall
shew me the truth of your articles,
and the falshood of mine, as hath
been said before, I am ready forth-
with

with to acknowledge my errour, &
to embrace your faith. But remember, I pray you, your promise, that
you would by the pure word shew
the truth of your faith and my errours; and that I renounced all antiquity, Councels, Miracles, Inhibitions, Lawes, visions vppon these termes only, and no other. Looke that
in steed of the pure word, you do not
shift me of with your interpretations or your owne consequences, for
either that interpretation is in the
Scripture, or no; if it be there, bring
forth the Scripture : and that the
Scripture saie of each proposition
you interprete, that it is so to be vnderstood, & that you only are the organe to pronounce the same, otherwise you leaue your owne faith and
forge an other to your owne liking,
of whic I shall argue with you after in the like sorte ; & besides that
you breake your promise. I should
be esteemd of small iudgment if I
forsake Councells, Miracles, Anti-
B   quity

quity and the rest for your interpretation.

If the Minister pretend to warrant his interpretation by some other passage of the Scripture, for example if he vrge that those words (*This is my body*) must not be taken properlie but figuratiuelie, because these others (*I ame a Vine*) haue such a signification : You shall aske him.

1. Before you passe to any interpretatiõ, if he haue any plaine text, which abstracting from all interpretation doth condemne vs of errour: for example in that point of the B. Sacrament, in which we beleeue there is the true body of our Sauiour. If he haue any, lett him bring that which is cleare and plaine, and leaue that which is obscure : if he haue none, make him to confesse distinctly, that he hath no place out of the pure word, by which, without his interpretation, he can conuince vs of errour; and heere you must insist

fift on this point, till he haue con-
feſſed this. After this Confeſſion
comming to the interpretation he
giues, you shall.

2. Demaunde, if the Scripture
fay that thefe words (*This is my Body*)
are to be interpreted by thefe (*I am
a Vine*) or no. If it fay fo, lett him
shew the place; If not, then the Miniſter breaks his couenants, & doth
not ſerue as an organe of the Scripture only. And heere the Miniſter is
in little eafe, neither can he, without renouncing their Confeſſion,
which profeſſeth to allow of nothing to rule them, but pure Scripture, paſſe any farther. Neither is it
needfull to purſue the matter anie
farther, this being concluded, for
heere haue you the Miniſter in the
ſtocks; and perchaunce it will be
better to keepe the Miniſtre in this
traunce ſpeechles, then to paſſe farther. Yet if you deſire an other victory, & that he, which encountreth
the Caluiniſt, be learned or expert

in the Scripture, he may, after the confession of the two former.

3. Harken to the interpretation the Minstre brings, and aunsweare these proofes he alleageth for that interpretation. But allwaies remember that the Caluinist, by their Confession of faith, is come to instruct vs, & consequently bound to prooue his interpretation; for vs, if it conuince not, it sufficeth to deny, without obligation to giue any reasons for our deniall: for by those the Minister will finde meanes to slippe away, and will not be so quicklie caught: he will seek many by-waies, therfore as much as may be stoppe his passage. Behold how you are to proceede, when the Minister vndertakes to shew our pretended errours by text of Scripture, without consequences or illations.

When he will discouer our errours by some consequence, which he deduceth out of the pure word of God: for example, ve beleeue that *the body*

oj

of our Lord is in the B. Sacrament of the Altar : he will prooue by conse-quence deduced out of the pure and sole Scripture, that he is not there, after this manner. In the 3. of the Actes, it is said, that *Heauen must con-teine him vntill the Consummation of the world*, therfore he is not on the earth. Behold his sillogisme. *That body which is in heauen is not on the earth, the body of Iesus Christ is in heauen, therfore it is not on the earth.* He must put his argu-ment in this forme. 1. Before you come to aunswere his argument, you must aske the Minister if he haue any plaine text, which without con-sequence doth condemne vs of er-rour in this point, or no ? If he haue, lett him bring it out, who professeth to reforme vs by the pure word ; If he haue not, make him confesse that he hath no plaine text, by which (his consequence (sett a part) we are con-uinced of errour ; & heere you must stay, and exact this confession of the Minister before you passe farther.

Ha-

Hauing made the Minister acknowledge this, though you may content your self with this victory (whereby you make him renounce the 5. article of their Confession of faith, and haue ouerthrowen that piller which detaines most of the Sectaries, who follow that part in their errours; who imagine they haue on their side the pure word of God, and that they builde vpon the Scripture only) and peraduenture it wil be better to proceed no farther, to the end to make it eccho oftener in the eares of these who are abused by them: Neuerthelesse he that will continew the chace, and hauing rowzed the deere from his lodge pursue him farther.

2. Giuing the Minister leaue to deduce his consequence, after the deduction thereof, the Catholicque must not straight examine the truth of the same, nor shew so quickly that it is false; but first lay hold on him, and make him shew, that his consequence is deduced out of the only pure

pure word of holy Scripture, as he promissed to deduce the same, and his 5. article doth oblige him. You must therfore proceede in this fashion. It is a thing vndoubted, and knowen to all, that euery consequence, to be good, must be inferred out of two propositions ; If then one of those two, out of which the Minister deduceth his consequence, be not in the Scripture, (as it happeneth ordinarily in the arguments of the aduersary against vs) heere you must demurr, and make it manifest, that the aduersarie heere abandonnes his Confession of fayth, and fayles of his promisse , in not shewing our pretended errour by cõsequence deduced out of the pure and only Scripture. For example, in the syllogisme before sett downe. *That body which is in heauen is not on the* *earth , the body of I Ius Christ is in heauen ,* *therfore it is not on the earth* : you shall examine the Minister, whether the first proposition of this argument be

in

in the pure word, or no. If it be, lett
him shew it. Cleere it is, it is not
there, but it is a philosophicall proposition, wherfore the Minister,
which deduceth his consequence
out of that, and the second adioyned, which is in the 3. of the Actes,
doth not proue my errour by consequence deduced out of the pure
word, but by consequence deduced
out of Philosophy, and out of the
word of God, and maketh such articles of faith, as are deduced out of
Philosophy or Aristotle. 2. You must
declare, that euery consequence
must be deduced out of two propositions, placed in the true forme of
a syllogisme, and that the consequence is inferred both from the
propositions, and from the forme
of the syllogisme; of which forme
the Scripture speakes nothing, nor
prescribes any rules about that matter, but only Aristotle, and Philosophy Wherfore the Minister in proouing his consequence, is not founded

ded vpon the Scripture alone, which
treates not of formes of consequences. And because it belongs to Aristotle, to iudge if the consequence
be good or no, the Minister building
vpon consequence, must admitt for
his iudge, in the controuersies of
our fayth, not the pure Scripture,
but Aristotle: or els at least choose
for vmpyre in this cause the word of
God, together with Aristotle. 3. You
must demaund of the Minister, if the
Scripture do teach that one must
beleeue as an article of faith, not
only that which the Scripture faith,
but also that, which by necessary
consequence followeth therevpon,
or no? if he say so, make him shew
the text, which without doubt
he cannot throughout the whole
bible: if no such be founde, then
doth the Minister build his articles
of fayth vpon a proposition, which
is not in the pure word, to witt v-
pon this. *That that which followeth out
of Scripture by necessary consequence, must*

B 5   *be*

be beleeued as an article of faith. Howbeit the Scripture frames no such
article, but the Minister only, and
that not by the pure Scripture, but
by humane reason : from which
notwithstanding in his c. Article he
disclaimed wholy. For he wold haue
vs take at his handes for an article
of faith that proposition, which by
consequence followeth out of the
Scripture, though the termes of
that proposition, deduced out of
Scripture for an article of fayth, be
not there sett downe. Hence is it
that all the articles of the Confession of these sectaries, which are
founded vpon a consequence, are
not articles of fayth, being that they
haue not for them theyr only rule
of truth, the sole Scripture. Heere
againe you must hold him. They
will say perauenture that I E S V S
Christ, and the Apostles proued many thinges by consequence. I graunt
it. But in so doing, they themselues
made new Scriptures, or holy writet
which

which priuiledge I thinke the Minister haue not. But they neuer
taught that the Scripture, which
they alledged, was the singular and
sole rule of all truth, and that they
spake not but by the mouth of the
Scripture, as these Pretenders professe, and thyr poore flocke (which
thinke they are as good as theyr
wordes) persuade themselues.

3. If he that buckle with the Minister be learned, and will, after he
hath often driuen the deere from his
fortresse of the pure worde, course
him alonge the plaine champion of
humane and philosophicall reasons
(though, according to my aduise,
it be ordinarily more expedient, to
content our selues with that before
sett downe) for to cure him, if it be
possible, after the aboue said he may
passe to the examen of the truth, or
falshod of his consequence: whether the propositions, from which
it is deduced (be they taken from
philosophy or holy writt) be true
or

or false; and whether the forme of the argument be according to the rules of Philosophy, and so deny that which the Minister assumed faisly. Still hauing in minde that the Minister is putt to the proofe, not the Catholick, who beares the personne of the party instructed; & be sure not to change that personne. For the drift of all the Ministers fetches is, to vnload himself of that obligation to prooue his consequence: which he will bring to passe by this sleight, if he can make him, that defends, the disputant. For example. In the argument proposed. *That body which is in heauen, is not on the earth; The body of Iesus Christ is in heauen; Therfore it is not on the earth.* You shall deny the first proposition, and lett the Minister prooue it. If that his proofes come on to long, & he enter to farre into Philosophicall quiddities, lett the Catholicke note that it is in his free choice, to curbe the Minister short when he listeth;

demaun-

demaunding him, if all the propositions which he hath brought to
prooue his conſequence, be in the
Scripture, or no. If they be, lett him
bring them forth . Many of them
queſtionles are drawne out of Phi-
loſophy, or grounded vpon humane
reaſons. If they be not, the Miniſter
which out of them inferres his conſequence, doth not deduce it out of
the pure word, or (which is all one)
prooues not by conſequence deduced out of the pure and only word,
that the Catholicke erreth, which
was that he vndertooke ; and moreouer denieth his Côfeſſion of faith :
for he drawes his côſequence ioynt-
ly out of the word of God, and out
of diuers propoſitions which are
not in holie write. Is not this to
flinch from their worde, and to renounce their articles of faith? or rather do not the Miniſter & his confeſſion of faith abuſe people, in promiſing that which they neither do,
uor canne performe.

Be-

Behold a breefe, and easy methode
to encounter all Ministers and Sectaries. Is it not obuious euen for
those, who are not students in deuinity, to putt it in practise? There
needs no more but eyes to see, and
to vnderstande English, to know if
the pure word without additions,
interpretations, or consequences of
others, do say such a thing, or no.
Do you not by this meanes euidently perceaue, that all the Ministers are
abusers, and how the whole troope
of Sectaries is misledde? Yea I dare
say double abusers. For first, the Minister abuseth men, in that he promiseth by the pure word to shew
them that, which he would haue
them beleeue: next, that he will by
the pure word lay open their errours
pretended, and yett performeth neither the one, nor the other. Wherfore the Ministers promising in their
31. and 5. articles to performe them
both, and yet effecting neither, as by
the forsaid practise is made euident;
are

are impostours, and double impostours: as this methode, which euery
Catholick may vse, doth apparently
declare. And so I haue fulfilled my
promise, which was to lay downe a
short and easie methode, by which
all Catholiques may euidently shew
that each Minister in all, and euery
point of his pretended religion, is an
abuser, & consequently that all their
followers are abused.

This therfore is my aduice to all
Sectaries, to those especially which
seeke sincerly theyr Saluation. Your
Confession promiseth you the pure
word of God, and you suppose that,
according to that promise, there is
nothing in your articles of fayth,
which is not in the pure word; Practise this methode, and you shall
euidently, and easily perceaue how
you are abused. Place on the one
syde the Principall articles of your
faith, which I haue cited before.
*That original sinne remaines after Baptisme
as it is a fault. That Iesus Christ is our*
only

only Aduocate. That faith alone iustifieth,
and which is cheefe of all. *That the B.
Sacrament is a figure of the body of our Sauiour, which is eaten by faith.* Then o-
uer against each of these articles, set
downe the textes, which are cited
in the margent for eache of them
(doubtles if you had any plaine text
of Scripture , which taught that
which is in that article, it wold haue
been coated in the margent) & you
shall cleerly see, that the pure word,
setting aside interpretations, and
Ministeriall consequences, hath not
that which is in your article: neither
is there required ought but your
eyes, and skill to reade, to see whether that be in the pure word or no.
And that your Ministers preach,that
the Scripture is easie, and that euery
one there may learne his owne saluation ; you vnderstand I ame sure
signification of English: why then
finde you not in the pure word that,
which the Ministers make you beleeue? Assure your selues if you find
it

it not, it is becaule it is not there.
Confront therfore the place cited
in the margent of the article, with
the article, and you shall lee how
egregioufly you are mocked. And
that you may lee this more manife-
ftly, doe this following. Write in
one line one article , or if it haue
many partes, one only claufe of the
fame. And if you finde any text of
Scripture cited for that article, or
peece therof, write in a fecond line
the words of the text cited, vnder the
other line. If you find no text cited
(as in many places there is not) put
vnder the firft line a cypher; for that
if there were any text to authorize
that article, it would be cited. This
being donne, compare the firft line
with the fecond : If you find in the
fecond line a cypher, you are cleerly
cofened. If you find a text of Scripture, fee if that, being precifely taken, without medly of fome thing
els (that is to fay, *you muft vnderft-*
ande ; *this fignifieth*; *or the like* ;) con-
taine

taine that article propofed ; if it do
not, know that you are deceaued.
I my felf haue paralelled thefe articles with the textes alledged in the
margent ; take you but the like
paines, and I will affure you that in
fteed of the pure word, you shall oft
tymes finde a cypher ; other tymes
in the text cited you shall not find
one worde of the article ; and in
breefe you shall not find there one
article, or entiere claufe of thofe in
Controuerfy between vs. Behold
how you are deluded.

ARTI-

ARTICLES OF THE
CONFESSION OF FAITH OF
the pretended reformed Churchs,
confronted with the pure word of
holy writt; Where it is euidently
shewed, that the textes of Scripture, euen in the Geneua Bible, cited in the margent of these articles, conteine nothing of that,
which those articles teach against
the Catholick faith.

Which is

A breefe & easy meanes, by which euery
Caluinist may manifestlie perceaue
how he is abused, and wherby each
Catholicke may shew the same vnto
him.

To saue you the paines (deceaued
Countrymen) which I wished you
to take, I haue heere confronted the
articles of your faith controu rted,
with the places cited in the marger,
after the fashion before sett downe,
and

and haue cited thefe textes according to the Geneua tranflation .
Compare them with tne beginning
at the 24. article.

In this article , thefe claufes following are fett downe without any
text, cited in the margent, for proof
of any of them; wherfore in fteede of
Scripture, I wil giue you vnder euery
claufe for proofe a Cypher.

Article 24.

1. *VVe hold that Purgatory is an
   Illufion.*

   Proofe.   o.

2. *By the abufe and deceipt of Sathan, Monaſticall vovves
   vvere introduced.*

   Proofe.   o.

3. *Out of the fame vvare-hovvfe
   proceeded Pilgrimages.*

   Proofe.   o.

4. *Out of the fame vvare-hovvfe
   vvas brought in Auricular
   Confeßion.*

   Proofe.

Proofe. o.

5. *Out of the same vvare-hovvse*
   sprang Indulgenees.

   Proofe. o.

6. *Out of the same vvare-hovvse*
   proceeded all other things, by
   vvhich vve thinke to merite
   grace and saluation.

   Proofe. o.

7. *VVe reiect all others meanes,*
   vvhich men presume to haue,
   to reconcile themselues to
   God, as derogatory from the
   death, and passion of Iesus
   Christ.

   Proofe. o.

8. *It is lavvfull for vs to pray but*
   only according to that forme,
   vvhich God sett dovvne in
   his vvord.

   Proofe. o.

In the 31. article you say. *The e-*
state

State of the Church in our times vvas interrupted, and hath failed ; that God hath raised some after an extraordinary manner to renevv the same, being ruinated and desolate.

Proofe. o.

Behold how the Ministers, and theyr Confession of faith do abuse you, and how often in one only article. They promise you, not to instract you but by the holy Scripture, and proposing vnto you all these clauses to be beleeued, they prooue none of them by any text of Scripture, nor bring as much as one place of Scripture for confirmation of them. Examine the articles, you will finde more then a hundred clauses as well affirmatiues, as negatiues, for proofe wherof there is no text coated, because in deed they haue it not, iudge then if you b abused or no.

Ans

And who, I pray you, can in equity accuse another, vnles he produce some lawe commaunding, or prohibiting some thing violated by the party accused? Euery accusation, commended to be truly an accusation, not a calumny, must be founded vpon the breach of some lawe, and accompanied with it proofes. These Reformers doe not only accuse, but making themselues iudges, doe condemne of Superstitions, forgery, and high treason against the deuine Maiesty, the holy Fathers, and vs all besides in those 8. poyntes sett downe (and in diuers others which I omitt) pronouncing theyr bloody sentence, by which they declare both them and vs to be superstitious, deceauers, instruments of sathan in the promulgations of those diuelish illusions rehearsed. This sentence pronounced, for execution of the same they haue ouerthrowen our Monasteries ; prophaned our holy places ; and set fire on our Churches.

Churches. Of what crime doe they accuſe vs, do they condemne vs? what deuine law doe they prooue to haue ben violated by vs? They neyther prooue, nor ſo much as cite any law, any letter of holy write, againſt which the holy Fathers & we haue offended. And yet they accuſe vs, they condemne vs. Shameles wretches! but yet withall impudent liars! They promiſe, not to behaue themſelues but only as inſtruments of the holy Scripture, and not to propoſe ought but that; And yet they pronounce the eight forſayd ſentences, without citing one ſole paſſage of the Scripture. See, o you ſectaries, how palpabl they abuſe you. But to ſee this more cleerly, and withall to take away from the Miniſters all meanes to circumuent you to your vtter ruine

Conſider with like attentii that which enſueth. In the 5. art cl they wold make you beleeu *that the pure word, which is conteined*

the bookes of *holy Scripture, is the rule of all truth*, and that nothing muſt be beleeued, but that which is in the pure word . This article is of great conſequence ; for repoſing and grounding your ſelues vppon this, and not vppon any other thing, you reiect all the traditions of the Romane Church ; you giue your ſentences of condemnation againſt vs ; you will not allow of *neyther Antiquity*, *nor Cuſtome, nor Multitude , nor Humane wiſedome, nor Sentences, nor Inhibitions, nor Edicts, nor Lawes, nor Councells, nor Viſions, nor Miracles*. And albeit all theſe make againſt your doctrine, you make no bones thereof, you ſcorne them all, ſaying that you will nothing but the pure Scripture, all the reſt proceeds from men ſubiect vnto errours ; and *that all other things muſt be examined, ruled, and reformed according to the ſame pure word.* This article therfore is of great conſequence ; and with good reaſon, to be beleeued, ought to be found in
C   the

the holy Scripture; which if the Ministers should frame in the force of
their owne braynes, they deserue
doubtles to be banished all honest
company, as men impudently bold,
which seeke to make the world renounce all things abouesaid, for a
proposition of their owne inuention; and contradict themselues:ha-
uing before said, they would only
carry themselues as the organe of
the wholy Scripture.Let vs therfore
set downe in one line first the article, then vnder that the text, cited
in the margent for proofe thereof.

Article 5.

The vvritten vvord is the rule of
all truth : or els, as you commonly say. *Nothing is to be be-*
leeued, but that vvhich is in the
vvritten vvord. In the margent of this article you cite
4. textes for proofe of the
contents.

I.

1. Text.

You shall not add any thing to the vvorde vvhich I commaunde, nor take any thing from the fame. Saith Moyfes to the people of Ifrael. *Deuter. 4. Verf. 2.*

2. Text.

That vvhich I commaund you, that shall you doe, neither shall you adde any thing, nor diminish. Deut. 12. Verf. 32.

Examen.

Heere is not any worde of the article in thefe paffages, for you neyther finde (*written word*) nor (*rule of all truth*) which are the two termes of the article; wherfore this pure word doth not conteine that, which the article affirmeth. Lett vs weigh it more exactly. 1. Moyfes fpake vnto the Iewes of that only, which he ordained, to witt of the Iudaicall law, and of no other. 2. he fpake not

C 2   of

of the written worde, of which
alone the article is, but vniuerfally
of the word. 3. Albeit he fpake vnto
Chriftians, and of the only written
word: haue we increafed the bookes of Moyfes ? haue we added
ought vnto them ? 4. Thinke you
that the *Prophets* compofing new
Scriptures, and ioyning them with
the bookes of Moyfes, haue infrin-
ged this precept? 5. if Moyfes for-
bid to beleeue any thing but that,
which he ordayned; we muft neyther beleeue the Pfalmes of Dauid,
nor the other *Prophets*, nor the Ghof-
pell: for he ordained not that which
thefe conteyne. Perceaue you not
how ridiculous a thing it is, to alledge this text, to verify by the pure
word your article? which fayth, *the
written word is the rule if all truth*. The
fame article is prooued by an other
paffage. Galat 1. Verf. 8.

3. Text.

*Although vve, or an Angell from
heauen*

*heauen preach othervvise, then
that vvhich vve haue preached
vnto you, be he accursed.*

Examen.

In this text I neither read (*written word*) nor (*rule of all truth*)which
are the two termes of the article;
wherefore the text hath not that,
which the article teacheth. Nay it
containes not one only word therof,
come to the examen. 1. Is there in the
text anie mention of the written
word? of which onlie we dispute,
and the article speakes of no other.
2. Who knoweth not that the Apocalipse was reuealed, and writt after
that epistle of S. Paule? and yet besides that, which S. Paule euangeli-
zed, it also must be beleeued. Or is
he which preacheth, and beleeueth
the Apocalipse accursed? Or rather
is S. Paule accursed, who preached
manie things afterward, which are
not in that epistle to the Galathians?
who is there of so small capacitie,

that

that in the reading of this chapter
doth not see, that the word (*otherwise*) is the same in sense with (*a-
gainst*.) The Apostle, as it is manifest at the verie opening of the epistle, crieth out against those, which
togeather with the law of Christ,
would ioyne Circumcision against
the doctrine of the Apostles. The
wordes immediatlie going before,
make the matter more cleere. *I mar-
uaile* saith he to the Galat: 1. Vers. 6.
7. 8. *that leauing him, who hath called
you vnto the grace of Christ, you are so
soone transferred vnto an other Ghospell:
which is not another, vnles there be some
that trouble you, & will inuert the Ghospell of Christ: But although we, or an Angell from heauen preach to you otherwise
then that, which we haue preached to you,
be he accursed.* Is it not euident that
S. Paul reiecteth that only, which is
against that which he had preached?
Then it is apparent also, that this
text makes nothing for that, which
the article contains, to witt: *That
the*

the written word is the rule of all truth.

The laſt paſſage, cited for the for-ſaid article, is out of the Apocalipſe 22. Verſ. 18. in theſe wordes.

4. Texte.

I teſtifie to euerie one, hearing the vvordes of the prophecie of this booke. If any man shall add to theſe things, God shall adde vppon him the plagues vvritten in this booke. And if anie man shall diminish of the vvords of the booke of this prophecy, God shall take avvay his part out of the booke of life, and out of the holy Citty, and of theſe things that be vvritten in this booke.

Neither do I reade in this paſſage (*written word of the entire Bible*) of which only the Article intreats, nor (*rule of all truth*) wherfore the text ſayth not, *that the pure word of the entire Bible is the rule of all truth,* as the Article auerreth, rather the text

C 4   con-

consents not in one only terme with
the article. Examine it. 1. Is it not
manifest, that S. Iohn spake not but
of the word conteyned in the Apocalipse ? which the Ministers will
not allowe to be the rule of all
truth ; to what purpose then for
proofe of that Article, *That the pure
word of the entire Bible is the rule of all
truth, do* they bring out this text? 2.
if S. Iohn sayd, that nothing must
be added to that word of the Apocalipse in this sense, and after this
Ministerial paraphrase (*that nothing
must be beleeued which is not therin contained*) then he which should beleeue the Ghospell, the Epistles of S.
Paul, of S. Iohn, and others, and the
old testament, should be accursed.
Where were the Ministers witts,
thinke you, when to proue that nothing must be bleeued, but that
which is in the Bible, they alledged
this passage ? 3. To adde to the Apocalipse, is to thrust in somthing as
part of that sacred booke: doe we
                                  doe

doe so? What frantik people are your
Ministers? and you, o Caluinists?
how grossely doth your Confession
of fayth abuse you, which treats
you in such a fashion, as if you had
not eyes to reade, nor iudgment to
vnderstand the signification of one
pure text? How many Ministeriall
glosses ar heere wanting, to make
these textes speake that, which this
article contaynes? Lett vs go on.

Whence haue you, that the bookes of the old and new Testament
are holy Scripture? how know you
that these bookes are Canonicall?
By the inward persuasion of the holy Ghost,
so you aunsweare in the 4. article
*That he makes vs decerne them from other
Ecclesiasticall bookes.* It is not then by
the holy Scripture that you know
this, for your inward persuasion is
not the written word. Consequen-
tly it is false, *That the pure word is the
rule of all truth, and that all things must
be examined, ruled, and reformed by the
same.* For it is not the rule of this verity;

C 5

rity, and that of greatest conſequence : to witt, that the bookes of
the old and new Teſtament are canonicall, and writen by deuine reuelation. Again, to reiect any booke
from the number of the Canonicall
(as for example you doe reiect that
of Tobias, and admitt the Ghoſpell of S. Mathew) you guide not
your ſelues by this rule of the pure
word, but, as you giue it out, of the
inward perſuaſion of the holy
Ghoſt. See how your articles deſtroy
each other. Tell me farther. Do you
hold that one may, and ought to
baptize little infants ? That we muſt
not rebaptize · hereticques, which
haue been baptized in the name of
the B. Triniry ; that we muſt keepe
holy ſunday, and not ſaturday ; you
beleeue that the Mother of God re-
mayned alwayes a virgin. Not-
withſtanding you finde not one text
of Scripture, to iuſtify any of theſe
points ; why do you then contradict
your ſelues and your article, which
tea-

teacheth, *that the written word is the rule of all truth.* Doth not S. Paul in the. 2. to the Theſſalon. 2. verſ. 15. exhort ſaying. *stand, and hold faſt the inſtructions* (our tranſlation reads traditions) *which you haue learned eyther by our word, or by our epiſtle.* Note that he makes mention of the word beſides that, which is written in Scripture ; and in the 2. to Timothe. 2. Verſ. 2. *The things which thou haſt heard of me by many witneſſes, theſe commend to faythfull men, which shall be fit to teach others alſo.* Doe not you perceaue a diuine word, taught not by writing, but by word of mouth ? In the. 1. to the Cor. 11. Verſ. 34. *Other things I will ſet in order when I come.* Such ordinances by word of mouth, are they not as well deuine as thoſe, which are ſett downe in writing ? I omit many other authorities to this purpoſe, by the way only citing theſe, for that it is not my intent to iuſtify, and prooue vnto you in this treatiſe that, which

we

we beleeue. My only scope is to
shew vnto you, that you are abused,
and that the pure word teacheth no
such thing, as your articles report.
This haue I performed in this article, which I haue examined with
the textes cited for the same ; for
the Article saith, that the written
word is the rule of all truth ; and in
the passages alledged, we neyther
read *written word*, nor *the rule of
all truth*. Wherfore they haue not
that which the article saith, otherwise, knowing to reade, we should
see it there. For conclusion heereof
the Caluinists, in this article of greatest importance, are therefore abused, and by consequence in all the
rest I before marked, which are out
of this deduced against vs ; which
are in great number. Reuew them,
and in so many points acknowledg
your selues deceaued.

I haue at large examined this article, aswell for that ; as hath been
shewed, it is of greatest importance;

as

as also for that the falshood therof
being difcouered, the Ministers are
bereaued of the most efficatious, and
ordinary meanes they had to defend
themfelues, in thefe conflicts; for
they alwayes fly for refuge to this
Propofition, *That nothing must be be-*
leeued, but that which is in the Scripture
Their cuftome is to queftion vs,
where finde you Purgatory in the Scrip-
ture? or *the reall prefence of the body of*
Iefus Chrift in the facrament of the Altar
&c. For, fay they, *if it be not there, it is*
fuperftition to beleeue it. And by this
meanes, in lieu of reforming our
pretended abufes by the pure word,
they cunningly engage vs to prooue
our faith. A wyly deuife. Catholicks
looke vnto their fingers, and be fure
that when they make you fuch que-
ftions, you take not vppon you to
be difputants : but allthough you
haue many authorities, yett bring
no place of Scripture to iuftify your
caufe. Marke well the wilines of
the Aduerfaries . They are bound
by

by their.31.article to reforme vs,and
by their.5.to do it by the pure word:
by this disguise and faire apparence
drawing many to their part. But
their practise is after another fashion. For knowing well that they
are neuer able to performe that,
which they haue bound themselues
vnto, to disingage themselues from
this obligation, by a fine deuise they
endeuour to make vs the plaintifs,
questioning vs after the fashion a-
foresaid. And if in awnswere of
their questions, you bring some expresse textes for your self, behold,
by this the Minister hath gott his
neck out of the coller, and hauing
before hand quitt himself of all An-
quity, Fathers, Miracles &c. he will
turne of the Scripture at his owne
pleasure, and in fine delude you,
though you haue ten cleere textes
for your purpose: Of this we haue
dayly experience. Handle him in an
other fashion. You must neuer lett
him change his coate. He is obliged
by

by the Confession of his faith to
shew you by the pure word your errours ; hold him to it there to his
testimonies of the pure word,
which must sett downe your pretended errours; Doe but this, and
I warrant you the Minister will
quickly be brought vpon his knees;
and haue a care you release him not,
but keepe him downe. But how ?
vrge him still with this, that he shew
you some expresse text of Scripture
which sayth, *That there is no Purgatory*;
or *That, the body of Iesus Christ is not in
the Eucharist*. It is his charge to do it,
who hath pawned his word to shew
vs by the pure word our errours. But
if he hope to scape the torture by
this sleight, saying that he sufficiently sheweth our errour in that (as he
sayth) we cannot shew by the
Scripture Purgatory, or the reall
presence : Haue a care, that though
you haue many cleere textes on
your side, bring none, make not
your selues Plaintifs, for so he will
be

be deliuered from the rack ; but
preſſe him eagrely that he shw you
that he promiſed, or at leaſt, *that nothing muſt be beleeued but that, which is
in the Scripture* (for by this maxime
alone doth he argue you of errour)
And then that after he hath donne
this, you will produce your places.
Not being able to shew this propoſition in the whole Scripture (as by
the precedent examen I haue shewd
he cannot) he is driuen to a non plus,
nor hath he any meanes to ſcape a-
way. Thus shall you shew breefly &
euidently, that their 31 and 5 articles
ar falſe, which promiſed to reforme
our pretended abuſes by the pure
word, and cannot do it : And that
the Mimiſters are egregious impoſtours, which vnder ſuch a faire pretext haue ſeduced ſo many thow-
ſands of ſoules. And you of the pretended religion, put but your Miniſters to this triall, and you will ſee
them preſently fall ſpeechles , and
your ſelues apparently abuſed.

Before

Before we paſſe any farther, I cannot omitt to examine breeflie one clauſe of the 24. article, which I before let paſſe, for that for it there is cited in the margent a texte, which is not donne in the other clauſes.

An other clauſe of the 24. article.

Out of the vvare-hovvſe of the deuill, proceede the forbidding to marrie, and the free vſe of meates, and the ceremonious obſeruation of ſome daies.

Text.

In the laſt times certaine ſhalt depart from the faith, attending to ſpirits of errours, forbidding to marry, commaunding to abſtaine from meates, vvhich God created for the faithfull, to receaue them vvith thanks giuing, for euerie creature of God is good, and nothing to be reiected. 1. Timoth. 4. Verſ 3.

Exa-

Examen.

By this clause the Article seemes to reprehend the Catholicque Church, but wrongfullie. For, 1. shee forbids not to marrie, otherwise no Catholick could be married, but that he must breake the precept of the Church; shee onlie causeth that to be kept, which God in his Scriptures commaundeth: to witt, that men fulfill their vowes, and for this cause that Preests, and others which haue vowed chastity, and continencie, obserue their vowes, wherby it followeth that they may not marrie. Neither doth the text alledged say ought to the contrarie. 2. I admire the little iudgment of the Ministers; doe they thinke that the Physitians *commaunding* their patients *to abstaine from some meates* for a time to recouer their health, doe goe against the Apostle, and *teach a deuilish doctrine?*

I ame more amazed at the impudency of these men, whoe reading the

the prohibition of some meates made by the Apostles, gathered togeather in the 1. Councell. Act. 15. vers. 28. in these wordes *It hath seemed good to the Holy Ghost and to vs, to lay no further burden vppon you, then these necessary things.* Among other things *that you abstaine from bloud and that which is strangled.* They dare, abusing the text cited, say, not without execrable blasphemy, against the holy Apostles, and against the holy Ghost. *That from the ware-howse of the diuell proceedeth the prohibition of some meates* ; terming heereby the holy Ghost sathan, and the first sacred Councell of the Apostles, the ware-howse of the deuill, and theyr prohibition an abuse and illusion. S. Paul, which assisted at that sacred Councell, is farr of from censuring in that manner that precept, which he with the rest had decreed *to abstaine from certayn meates.* But forseeing that there wold come heretiques, that wold forbidde mariage as

a

a thing in it self vulawfull, and in-
uented by the deuill; and some
meates as naught in themselues and
of their owne nature (so did the
Maniche, Marcion and Tatian, as
S. Augustine, with others recoun-
teth)these the Apostle condemneth.
The Church is farr distant from this
errour. Thus doe S. Augustine, S.
Chrisostome, S. Hierome, and S.
Ambrose expound this place; and
the reason which the Apostle brin-
geth for his condemnation conteined in these words, *euery creature of
God is good*, doth authorize the same.
And it belongs to the Minister, who
is plaintife, to prooue the contrarie.
Finally, the Church doth not absolutelie commaund to abstaine from
meates, for it forbiddeth not fish,
whice is meate; nor at all times, but
onlie certaine particular meates, and
at certaine times; which thing the
Apostle reprehends not, who speaketh of these, who absolutelie *commaunde to abstaine from meates*, and that
with-

without limitation to any times. 3.
for the proofe of the 3. clause of the
obſeruation of daies, the article hath
cited no texte, in that therfore it de-
ceaueth.

An other clauſe of the 24. article.

*IESVS CHRIST is giuen
vs for the ſole Aduocate : All
that vvhich men haue imagined
about the interceſſion of Saintes
departed, is nought els but an
abuſe and deceipt of Sathan.*

Examen.

The onlie pointe of controuerſie
betwéen vs in the firſt clauſe of this
article, is of the word (*ſole*) for thes
two textes are cited in margent, for
the ſecond clauſe nothing, the firſt
in the 1. Timoth. 2. 5.

Texte.

*There is one only God, and
one onlie mediatour betvveen
God and men, man IESVS
CHRIST.*

Exa-

Examen.

I will set downe the texte entier-
ly, to make it more cleere that he
faith not that, which the article teacheth: behold the Apostles wordes.

God vvill that all men be sa-
ued, and come to the knovv-
ledge of truth, for there is one
only God, and one only media-
tour betvveene God and men,
man IESVS CHRIST vvho
gaue himselfe for reedmption of
all .

I finde not in this passage alledged the termes (*of Aduocate, of in-*
tercession) of which we debate, neither finde I thar Saints are shutt out
from that office of Aduocate, as
faith the article. And if the Minifter
fay that the name of mediatour, as
S. Paul vnderstands it, is the fame
with Aduocate; I aunfweare firft,
that the Minifter, or rather his Confeffion of faith, muft prooue that the
name

name of mediatour is taken for mediatour, and Aduocate by intercession, and not for mediatour and Aduocate by redemption; He I say
must prooue this, and that by the
pure word alone, otherwise the
place alledged consenteth not with
the Confession of faith, neither doth
it reiect the intercession of Saintes.
2. I make aunsweare (which by the
place entirely cited doth appeare)
that S. Paul spake of one Mediatour
(they are the Apostles owne words)
who *hath giuen himselfe a redemption*
for all: of such a Mediatour he saith
that he is one alone, neither doe the
Catholickes teach that the Saintes
are such mediatours. This passage
therfore prooues nothing against
Catholicques, neither doth it say
that IESVS CHRIST is giuen vs
for our sole Aduocate, nor that to
beleeue the intercession of Saints is
an abuse, and deceipt of the deuill.
3. This word (*sole*) hath beene added by the Ministers in the Geneua
Bible

Bible for it is neither in the Greeke
nor Latin texte : and S. Paule to the
Calat. 3. calleth Moyses Mediatour.

The seconde passage, alledged for
this clause in their Confession, is in
the 1. epistle of S. Iohn. 2. Vers. 1. 2.

2. Texte.

*These things I vvrite vnto
you, that you sinne not. But & if
any one sinne, vve haue an Aduocate vvith the Father, IESVS
Christ the iust : for he is the propitiation for our sinnes , and
not for ours only ; but also for
those of the vvhole vvorlde.*

Examen.

Is it not manifest , that he speaketh not of euery Aduocate, but of
an Aduocate which is a propitiation
for the sinnes of the whole world, to
witt by the effusion of his bloud?
The Catholicques hold not any o-
ther such Aduocate, but our Sauiour. To what purpose then is it to
bring

bring this passage, which toucheth not that which is in controuersie? And marke well that it is the Ministers parte, who is Plaintife, to shew that the name of Aduocate is heere taken for anie intercessour, euen him, who is not a propitiation for the sinnes of the world by his passion; and all this by the pure worde. 2. Besides, if the Minister will pertinaciously vnderstand by the name of Aduocate him, who is not a propitiation for the sinnes of the world (which is of his owne head without the pure word, yea against the pure word alledged.) This word (*only*) of which wee only striue, not being in this text, this place verefieth not this article *that IESVS Christ is only Aduocate.*

Let vs come to the 20. Article, These are the wordes.

Article. 20.

VVe beleeue that vve are made partakers of that iustice

D   (tc

(to witt Christian) *by faith alone.*

Textes cited in the Margent of this Article.

Man is iustified by faith vvithout the vvorkes of the lavve. Rom. 3. Verſ. 28.

Man is not iustified by the vvorkes of the Lavve, but only by the faith of I E S V S Chriſt. Galat. 2. Verſ. 16.

Before faith came vve vvere kept vnder the lavv, shut vp vnto that faith vvhich vvas to be reuealed. Therfore the lavve vvas our Pedagogue in Chriſt, that vve might be iustified by faith, but vvhen that faith is come novv vve are not vnder a Pedagogue. Galat. 3. Verſ. 23.

Examen.

I

I reade not one word, in all thefe textes, of the workes of Chriftian faith, of which alone, and of no o-thers we fpeake, and hold neceffary to iuftification. It is manifeft that this pure word alledged, fpeaketh of workes of the Iudaicall religion, ftyled commonly by S. Paul by the name of the Lawe, and not of the workes of Chriftian Religion. Thefe paffages therfore fay onlie, that Chriftian faith without Cir-cumcifion, and other ceremonies of the Iewes, doth iuftifie. Who de-nieth this? is this all one, or as much as to fay that Chriftian faith, with-out the workes, which proceed from the faid faith in Iɛsvs Chrift, as is penance, doth iuftifie? Which is that the article teacheth. Wher-fore this pure worde feconds not that which the article fayeth. I am amazed at the impudency, or igno-rance of the Minifters: S. Paul dif-courfing fo largely in fiue whole chapters of that epiftle to the Gala-

D 2   thians,

thians, against those which would
ioyne with Christian faith Circumcision, and other workes of Iudais-
me,; and the very titles of those
chapters in the Geneua transl tion
noting the same : yet the aduersaries
will alledge these against them, who
hold that Christian workes are necessarie to iustification. Open but
the epistle, and thou wilt detest such
abusers; the whole epistle sheweth
that which I say. It shall suffise for
proofe heereof to cite the words of
the. 5. chapter. 2. verse. *Behold I tell*
you, that if you be circumcised, Christ shall
proffit you nothing, and I testifie againe to
euerie man circumciding himself, that he
is a debter to doe the whole law ; you are
euacuated from Christ, that are iustified in
the law. You are fallen from grace, for
we by faith exspect the hope of iustice. In
IESVS Christ neither circumcision a-
uaileth ought, nor prepuce, but faith wor-
king by charity. Do not you falsefye?
doth not S. Paul teach in these laste
wordes the contrarie to your article ?

cle? The Apostle opposeth Christian
Religion, which is called faith in
Christ, vnto the Iudaicall religion,
which is named the lawe; and teacheth that this later is not necessary
to iustification, but that the former
suffiseth, and doth not oppose Christian faith to Christian workes. The
last texte cited for the foresaid article, hath as little energy as the precedents. it is this of S. Iohn 3. Vers.
15. 16.

> *As Moyses exalted the*
> *Serpent in the desert, so must*
> *the sonne of man be exalted,*
> *that euerie one vvhich belee-*
> *ueth in him, perish not, but*
> *may haue life euerlasting .*
> *For so God loued the vvorld,*
> *that he gaue his only begotten*
> *sonne, that euery one that be-*
> *leeueth in him, perish not, but*
> *haue life euerlasting.*

The word (only) of which only

is our variance, and which is in your
article, teaching that faith only iuſtifieth, is not in this text: wherefore this, vnleſ you add thereto the
word (*only*) makes nothing to your
purpoſe; and how often doth this
ſpeech, *to beleeue in IESVS Chriſt*, ſig-
nifie *to profeſſe the Ghoſpell, and liue according to the ſame?* for *faith*, ſaith. S.
Iames in the 1. chapter 17. verſe. *If
it haue not workes is dead.* Doth not S.
Paul. Galat. 5. Verſ. 6. ſay that *that
which iuſtifieth is faith, working by cha-
ritie?* Doth not our Sauiour pronounce this ſentence; if thou wilt
enter into life keepe the commaun-
dements? But I am not bound to
prooue, that faith alone without
Chriſtian workes doth not iuſtifie, it
is you that are engaged to prooue
by the pure worde, that that *alone*
doth iuſtifie; *alone*, I ſay, for of that
alone doe we diſpute. In the 11. article it is ſaid that.

Article 11.

Ori-

*Originall finne after Bap-
tifme is ftill finne, as it is a
fault; hovvbeit the condemnation thereof is taken avvay
in the children of God, vvho
of his mercifull goodnes doth
not impute it vnto them.*

In proofe of this is alledged one
only place in the margent. Rom. 7.
Verf. 7.

Texte.

*VVhat shall vve fay then?
is the lavve finne? God for-
bid, but finne I did not knovv,
but by the lavve, for concupif-
cence I knevv not, vnles the
lavv did fay, thou shalt not
couet.*

Examen.

Here is not in the text one word
contained in the article; wherefore
this Confeffion, promifing to fay
nothing but by the pure word, abu-

D 4   feth

seth'vs in this point. Go on.

Let vs examine the 36. and 37. articles, which speake of the B. Sacrament: which since it is obscurely spoken of, for more perspicuity I will borrow somewhat out of your Catechisme.

The 1. clause of the 36. article.

VVe testifie that the Supper is a testimonie of the vnitie, vvhich vve haue vvith I E-SVS Christ; vvhose body (you say in your Cate-chisme in the 53. lesson or Sunday) is not included vn-der the bread, nor his bloud vvithin the chalsce, that vve must not seeke him in these corruptible elementes. For proofe you alleadge this texte.

Text.
The cuppe of benediction vvhich

*vvhich vve do blesse, is it not
the communion of the bloud of
Chriſt? and the bread vvhich
vve do breake, is it not the
communion of the bodie of
Chriſt? for being manie, vve
are one only bread, and one
only body, for vve all partake
of one only bread.*1.Corinth.
10. Verſ.16.17.

Examen.

I reade not in this text (*teſtimony
of the vnity with I E S V S Chriſt*.) the
text therfore agrees not with the
article. But I reade *communion of
blond, communion of body,* which is a
different matter from *teſtimony of
vnity with I E S V S Chriſt*, and sheweth *that the body of I E S V S Chriſt
may be founde in theſe corruptible elements,* vnder the accidents of bread
and wine ; which this article de-
nieth.

An other clauſe of the ſame article.

In the supper are *signss, which te-stify that the body and bloud of IESVS Christ, serueth no lesse for the soule to eate and drinke, then bread and wine doth for the body.* These Articles say not in expresse termes that *the body of IESVS Christ is not in the Eucharist* to couer with obscurity theyr errour; to dis-perse this darknes I must borrow some light from theyr Catechisme in the 53. lesson. *we must not (sayth it) vnderstand that the body is inclosed within the bread, nor the bloud within the chalice; but contrariwise, to haue the verity of this sacrament, we must lift vp our hartes on high to heauen, where IESVS Christ is, and not seeke him in these corruptible elements.* For this clause you cite two textes.

1. Texte.

I am the liuing bread, that came dovvne from heauen: if any man eate of this bread, he shall liue for euer, and the bread vvhich I vvill giue is

my

my flesh, vvhich I vvill giue for the life of the vvorld. Iohn. 6. Verſ. 51.

Examen.

Firſt I reade not in this text (*ſignes which teſtify*) but this expreſſely, that *Chriſt is the liuing bread,* not co-mon bread made of flowre, and ba-ked ; but *which is his fleſh*, which ſayth he, *I will giue for the life of the world* ; As alſo in the geuing of it he ſayd, Take, *This is my body, which ſhal be giuen for you.* Was it a ſigne, or figure of his body, which was nayled one the croſſe : was it not his proper body? This clauſe then is falſe. 2. The miniſters, whoe haue promiſed to propoſe nothing but the pure Scripture, how doe they thruſt vppon vs this clauſe ſo wei-ghty, *The body of IESVS Chriſt is not contained, and included within the bread, nor the blood &c.* Without any writ-ten word? ſee theyr fraude, and how well they keepe theyr word
in

in a matter of greateſt moment.

2. Texte.

*I E S V S tooke bread, and
hauing giuen thankes brake
it, and ſaid take, eate. Thſ is
my bodie, vvhich is broken for
you ; do this in commemoration
of me. In like manner after
ſupper he tooke the cuppe ſaying, this cuppe is the newv teſtament in my blood, this do
ye, as often as you ſhall drinke
theraf in remembrance of me.*
1. Corinth. 11. Verſ. 24.

Examen.

Who can ſinde out in this texte.
*Signes which teſtify ; figure ; ſigne of the
body of I E S V S Chriſt ; which is not in
the bread, nor the blood in the chalice ?*
all which the article teacheth. The
text then helpes them nothing ; nay
how could the text more cleerly
reiect the aduerſaries beleeſe, which
is that the body is not vnder the bread,
nor

nor the bloud within the chalice. Let
the Caluinistes consider if they be
abused or no : The Ministers haue
entred bondes to shew by the pure
word, That the supper *is a signe which
testifieth, a figure of the body of our sauiour, which is not vnder the bread, and
of the bloud which is not within the chalice:*and to cancell theyr obligations,
they bring for paiment this texte of
Scripture,in which (being it is written downe) if you reade it not, eyther you want your sight, or they
deceaue you. Rather see you not
the contrary ? then say they are doubled iuglers.

An other clause of that Article.

After affirming that IESVS Christ
doth nourish, and quicken vs with
the substance of his body, and of
his bloud, that which the Catholickes beleeue also ; they add, (in
which we disagree) without aledging any texte for the same (wherefore put vnderneath for proofe a
cypher as before.)

I. Wo

1. *VVe hold notvvithstanding, that this is donne spiritually.*
Proofe. o.

2. *The supper is a figure of the body, or, In the supper is figured the bodie of IESVS Christ.*
Proofe. o.

3. *Because the misterie of this supper is celestiall, it cannot be taken but by faith,* or to vse their vulgar phrase, *by the mouth of faith : Those vvhich bring vvith them a pure faith as a vessell, receaue trulie that vvhich the signes testifie ;* commonlie they say, *That in the supper is eaten the bodie of IESVS Christ by the mouth of faith* and in the 53. Sunday of their Catechisme, it is said, *to haue the veritie of*

the

*the Sacrament, vve muſt lift
vp our hartes to heauen
vvhere it is.*

Proofe.　o.

Behold many articles, and of
greate conſeqnence proued by a
Cypher. Behold how you are abuſed. The miniſters make you beleeue
all this, not being able to shew for
it any texte of Scripture. The conſequence will be, that your ſupper
is purely their owne inuention :
This by your principles I shew. For
you haue no pure textes which ſay
that, which you affirmatiuely beleeue of the ſupper, of which you
hold thoſe three thinges aforeſayd
principally. *It is figure &c. that by the
mouthe of fayth the body eateh &c.* you
should diſtinctly ſett downe that,
which of our fayth you deny in this
matter, from that which therein you
poſitiuely beleeue : for how be it
that we did erre (of which I haue
shewed the contrary) and that your
nega-

negatiue propofitions *I ESV S Chrift is not in the Euchariſt, and the like* were true ; it followeth not that that, which you affirmatiuely beleeue, moſt needes be true ; and that you erre not therein. Becauſe one goeth wrong one way, is he, which takes an other, certaine to goe right ? may not both be out of their way ? Examine therfore your aſſertions, and you finde not any ſhew of textes that teache, *that the ſupper is a figure of the body &c.* nor which *ſpeake of the mouth of faith.* Confequently your whole ſupper is a humane inuention. Which being ſo, in my opinion in the eating a good capó, or a cock, you may more eaſely remember the death of the ſonne of God, for that therein is made mention of the crowing of a cock ; then in eating a bit of bread. For which cauſe you ſhall do more prudently, to make of them a figure & memorie, then of a peece of bread ; which is no more holie, then that you eate commonlie at

your

your table.

It may be that some Caluiniste, thinking himselfe better skilled in the Scriptures, then the Ministers which composed the Confession of faith, and cited for proofe therof those sacred textes they iudged most fauourable, will vrge, to prooue *the supper to be a figure*, that, which our Sauiour said Iohn. 6. Verl. 63. *It is the spirit which quickeneth, the flesh proffiteth nothing, the words which I speake vnto you are spirit and life.* For awnswere. 1. You must vnderstand, that your Ministers are at variance, whether in the 6. of S. Iohn anie thing be spoken of the supper. Caluin in the fourth booke of his Instit. cap. 17. §. 33. Kemnicius, and Zuinglius deny it. How then will you establish this firme article of your faith vpon so weake a foundation, doubted of by these of your owne faction? How can you serue your selues of that passage against vs, either for your figure, or for your *spiritually*?

2. I

2. I reade not in this text *figure* : and if anie one say that *spirit* and *figure* is all one ; I may not beleeue him without his proofe, and that by the pure Scripture. And who perceaues not how ridiculous this deuise is? the diuells are spirites, are they figures? the Angells and our soules are spirittes? are they also figures? God himself is he not a most pure spiritt? is he a figure? it belongs not to me to explicate this place. I only shew that the pure word saith not that, which the article conteineth, & consequently the Ministers mock vs. Yet by the way, knowe that the sense of this texte is, that our Sauiour would not giue vs to eate his flesh dead, and in peeces (as we eate of the ordinarie flesh, as the Caphar-naites imagined) to eate of flesh in this manner, proffitteth nothing to saluation ; but flesh animated by his spirite, and quickened by his deuine life : in this manner we eate it. In which fashion we cannot eate anie

other

other flesh, for it must first be dead, before it nourish vs. Remember finally that I doe not by this Scripture prooue my faith, this suffiseth me, that in these words you reade not *either figure of body, or that we hold that it is donne spiritually, in such manner that the body is not contained there*, this, I say, suffiseth to make you know you are misledd. For since you reade it not, (which doubtles if it were there, you might) the pure word warranteth not that which this article containeth.

Behold Syr the arte, which in this letter I promised to discouer vnto you : is it not a rare & worthy hunting-game ? haue you ere this seene such coursing ? F. Veron in teaching it me, told me that, which I know will giue it no small luster in your eye : that he receaued the origine, and substance therof from the R. F. Gontery, which famous hunter was the authour, and inuentour of this so efficacious, and facile sport; who also vsed no other in his disputes aagainst the Ministers, iudging this the best, and most powerfull of all. And you know well, that that fearfull scourge of the Hereticks, is most expert in these combats. And
being

being so beaten a soldiour in those warres, each prudent man wil make a great esteme of his aduise herein. He hath putt to slight the Ministers of Dieppe, of Caen, of Sedan &c. and among the rest some Allmaines he founde at Tourlac. But how? Truly by no other meanes but this, by the pure Scripture alone, and that after the Geneua Translation, by the practise before set downe: Sauing that he brideled them in more shortly, for he neuer suffered them in any point debated, to proceed by consequences, which they said they would deduce out of the Scripture, vnles they first subscribed, that they could not enter combate with vs by the pure written word.

I should now sende you the relation promised of this Conference, between F. Veron, and the Minister Hucher, but because the printer, by reason of the great frostes could not dispatch the same so soone, as I hoped; not to keepe you wholy in suspence, I send you the summary thereof, togeather with the meanes to buckle with the Sectaries. The whole Conference is vnder the presse, you shall haue it within eight daies; ioyne it to this fashion of hunting which I now send you, for in that you will see the practise of this kinde of chace, vsed by the Father in this conflict. Heere will you also see, by this so

suc-

successfull and remarkable victory, the
efficacy of this arte. It is scarcely possible
to putt a man to more confusion, then the
Minister was in. The fame of this victory
strooke the sectaries to the harte. Seeing
the title of this epistle before it was printed, they were much offended at it, but all
partes thereof are easily iustified, by the
Actes of the Conference signed. Behold
out of them the Ministers owne wordes.
He hauing promised to shew by the pure
word, that IESVS Christ is not in the Eucharist, after a little pressing said; *The truth*
is, that these vvords (the body of I E S V S
Christ is not in the Eucharist) are not in the
scripture. And after being vrged a little
harder, he confessed besides twice, before
all the assembly, that he had not any text in
Scripture, which, setting aside all consequences, conteyned formally and expres-
ly the sense of this proposition. *IESVS*
Christ is not in the Eucharist, which notwithstanding he before vndertooke to shew by
the pure word; and so to reforme the Iesuite in his errour. Is not this as much as
to confesse, that he could not by the pure
word reforme vs in this point? is not this
to forsake it? is not this to renounce the
office and exercise of a reformer? thinke
you these fittes proceede from a merry
hart? wherfore with reason the epistle
beares for title *The Minister of Amiens con-*
strained

strained to renounce the pure vvord of holy vvrite: He stayed so long dumme, and in presence of so many personnes, and of such quality, that there is no tergiuersation: and refused so long time in the third session, to come to the proofe of that, in which the day before he was struck speechles, or also to deale in any other point; that the flight is as euident, as the day light. VVherfore the epistle hath right vnto his title. VVithin few dayes you shall see the narration at large, well subscribed and signed; in the meane tyme notwithstanding, for iustification of the summary thereof, sett downe in the beginning of this letter, I haue procured thele subscriptions following.

Subscriptions of the Conference, the summe vvherof is contained in the beginning of this letter.

VVE the subsigned Gentlemen of the Duke of Longueuille, being present with our said Lord at the Conferences, of which the narration is before set downe, do testifie that they haue truly passed as it is declared. Giuen at Amyens the 12. of February. 1615.

Pelletot, Foucaucourt, Le Cheualier de Moyencourt, Gondreuille, Tannere, Gouftimenil, Courtauenel.

Certaine poincts collected out of this practise, and other experiences of this kind, reduced to six heads, for the more warie proceeding of Catholiques with Sectaries of our age.

THE 1. poinct. Seeing that our new Sectaries doe suppose vs Catholiques to be deceaued, in our beleefe, and that they ar sent to reforme vs by the *onlie written word of Scripture*, er the Catholique enter into conference with anie Sectarie, let him first demaund what he vnderstandeth by the *onlie written word of Scripture*: whither the Old and new Testament, with all the parts of eche both, as we Catholiques doe; or els what? Then let the Catholique request the Sectarie to proue by the *onlie written word*, as he tooke vppon him, that the whole Bible, or such parcels as he doth admit for holie Scripture, or reiect, ar in deede, or ar not holy Scripture. He cannot doe it; but by Tradition, and by the Catholique Church her authoritie.

The 2. is. No Catholique conferring, must seeke to proue our opinions, which the Sectaries disalowe of; for we ar in possession, and defendants, not plainetifes.

The 3. is. The Catholique must not in any case permit the Sectarie to bring anie proofe whatsoeuer, other then the *onlie written word of Scripture*, and this also, with without anie interpretation, glose, or conceance of his owne braine.

The 4. is Let not the Catholique suffer his Aduersary to leape from pale to pearch, and from one Controuersie to another ȳntill he be conuinced of errour in his beleefe, and this by the *onlie vvritten vvord.*

The 5 is. The Sectarie not proouing by the *onlie vvritten vvord*, that which he promised, is not able to performe it; the Catholique must constraine ether him, or some els there present, to subscribe that he could not prooue what he vndertooke in such sort, as he ought to haue donne.

The 6. and last is. The Catholique must confer, and confider with attention the places of Scripture, alledged by Sectaries to disproue our doctrine; for ordinarilie they make no more to the purpose, then peare to a nut For example to prooue *that vve must beleeue the onlie vvritten vvord* they bring forth these places. Deuter 4. v. 2. Deuter. 12. v. 32. Galat. 1. v. 8 Apocalip. 22. v. 18. which make nothing against vs, or for them. For by the first and second, we should, according to the sense of our aduersaries, beleeue nought els, but that which is in the Deuteronomie; by the third, nothing but that epistle of S. Paul; by the last, nought els but the Apocalipse. See theire madnes, and foolery, and looke to theire water.

A Dieu, and be well aduised.

LUKE WADDING

The History of . . . S. Clare
1635

THE HISTORY

OF THE ANGELICALL VIRGIN

GLORIOVS

S. CLARE,

DEDICATED TO THE QVEENS

MOST EXCELLENT MAIESTY.

EXTRACTED OVT OF THE R. F. LVKE
Wadding *his Annalls of the Freer Minors*
chiefly by Francis Hendricq *and now*
donne into English.

By sister *Magdalen Augustine*, of the
holy Order of the *Poore Clares*
in Aire.

Imprinted at DOVAY, by MARTIN BOCART
vnder the signe of Paris.

M. DC. XXXV.

TO THE MOST HIGH
AND MIGHTY PRINCESSE,
MARY HENRIETTE,
QVEENE OF GREAT
BRITAINE,
FRANCE AND IRELAND:
AND SOVVERAIGNE LADY
OF THE ILES OF THE
BRITISH OCEAN.

MAY it please your most gracious
Maiestie;

BEING *to publish to the view
of the* World, *the Life of the Mi-
rour and Princesse of Religious Foundresses* S. Clare; *and being, according to the Custome no lesse
frequented than laudable, to bethink our selues of
some grand Personage, vnder whose Protection it
might passe, it seemed to vs impertinent to entertai-
ne any long Consult, to that purpose, seeing your
Maiestie, did at the very first deliberation, occurre
to our thoughts, accompanied with many Titles
clayming to your matchles Excellencie, the Dedica-
tory addresse and Protection of the* Worke. *For first,
if* Wee *did contemplate the Royall and thrice renow-*

ned *Progenie* of France , *from whence your Ma-*
ieftie is extracted, it feemeth a thing proper, If not
hereditary, to that Princely familie, to be addicted to
thechildren of our Seraphical *Father,* S. Francis.
To whom *God communicated* Abraham's *priui-*
ledge (Genef. 12.) I will bleffe them that
bleffe thee and curfe them that curfe thee. *In*
fo much , as that great Honour of France, *and*
glory of Kings, S. Lewis *who (being by his Mo-*
ther, for her fingular Deuotion to our holy Father,
tendred to the Freers to be educated by them in
their Monaftery) fayd: *that yf he could part and*
diuide himfelfe in two, he would bequeath one part
of himfelfe to the Freers: but being he was not able,
for the important affaires of his Crowne, in fo ftrict
a manner to become a child of our holy Father, he
made himfelfe a Member of his Third Order; *for*
which reafon, he hath merited an immortall glory
in the Roll of the faints of that Order. and indeed,
what your Maiefties Deuotion hath been towards
S. Francis, *you haue yeelded fufficient proof and*
teftimonie thereof; when before your comming into
England (*as we are informed*) *together with your*
Royall Brother K. Lewis, *now prepotent Monarch*
of France, *you publikly at* Paris, *with him, re-*
ceiued S. Francis Cord, *a* Symbole *and* Reco-
gnifance *of the Sacred Paffion of our Souueraigne*
Redeemer, *for which this Sodalitie is enftiled the*
Arch confraternitie, *as hauing a more honorable*
Inftitution *and* Dedication *than any other Confra-*
ternitie what foeuer. Againe: *yf we propofed to our*
Confideration, *the fuperem inentie of this firft* Plant

of

of S. Francis, I *meane our holy Mother* S. Clare: *we shall find that she by singular* Preroga-*tiue of* Euangelicall Pouertie *, both in proper and in common,* (*which neuer any other Religious Foundreße profeßed before her:*) *merited to be in that eminent degree so espoused to her Lord Chrift Iesus though* Poore, *yet a* King, *that she must needs confequently also be* (*as we may so say*) *a* Princeße *and* Queen. W*hich being so, she would esteeme it an abridgment or disparagement to her Honour, to be recommended to the fauorable acceptance of any other than a* Queen: *and especially to such a one as we haue formerly delineated and reprefented.* Fi-*nally: if we did but set before our eyes the mani-fold starres of virtues, which tender this saint most illustrious, we shall find also your* Maiestie, *by a certaine femblance, to be also conspicuous for the va-rietie of your many perfections: enuironning and com-paßing your* Princely Robes. *Forshould we with* S. Bonauenture, Seraphical Doctour *of the* Church, *proclaime her* most endeared to God, the flo-wer of the Spring, yeelding a most fragrant odour, and a most refulgent bright-shining starre. *The fame* (*without offence*) *we would pro-portionably depredicate of your* Maiestie. *Ifrauished with her eminencie, we should breake forth, with* Pope Alexander *the* Fourth, *into that admira-tion,* O admirable glorie or Claritie of B. S. Clare, *which by how much the more* studi-ously in all things she is contemplated, by so much the more she appeares Cleare, Renow ned & Refplendent: *The fame admiration of your*

á   3   Highnes

The Epistle Dedicatory.

Highnes Excellencie imperfection, observing a due proportion, would we utter and promulge: did we not know your Maiesties Feminine *and Religious* Modestie, *not to delight to view the Register of your incomparable and indeed vnspeakables praises. And likewise, did we not vnderstand full well, that our* Profession *is not to celebrate (Rhetorically) or praise, but to pray incessantly.* We will therefore, euer pray the only Ruler of Princes, which hath set a Diademe of pure gold vpon your head, to preuent you with the blessings of his goodnes, and grant vnto your Maiestie a long and prosperous ioynt-reigne with our Soueraigne Liege-Lord, King Charles, *and a glorious* Race *from your* Royall loynes to the Crowne. The enioyance of which happines that you may, by the powerfull intercession of our All-Immaculate Lady, the Blessed Virgin Mary: his great seruant the Seraphicall Father, and the Angelicall Virgin our holy Mother S. Clare, (whose Life heer we prostrate in al humility, tender to your Gracious hands) which happines (we say) that your Maiestie may long heer, and in the future for euer and euer, in full possession obtaine, wee shall professe our vnworthy selues euer to be, and remaine.*

YOVR MAIESTIES

Most humble, and dayly
deuoted Beadf-women

The English poore-Clares
of Aire.

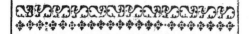

TO THE READER.

Entle Reader:
Loe heer presented to thy
view, the Life of a Saint; of *Feminine* Sexe, but *Masculine* Virtue. I will not, by fore speaking
Her praises, preuent the Book, but to prepare
thee, to reade it with better profit, is my present Dessigne. Thou mayst (haply) find therein
to please thy curiositie, and to polish thy vnderstanding; but the mortified *Recluse*, that trauelled in this Translation, had an ayme at thy
greater Benefit. God Almighty hath made His
Saints renowned for Virtue, that they might be
exemplary; and they which commended their
doeings to Posteritie, or do represent them to
the view of present tymes, wish this only Reward of their Industry, that others be excited
to the imitation of their Heroicke actions:
gladly aduenturing on the Censure of Many, yf
they may procure the spirituall comoditie of a
Few. Say not, I am vnwilling to walk this way;
for I am not bound to perfection: rather esteem
thy selfe bound, and deferre not thy endea-
uours to become perfect. It is true, their obli-

gation

gation this way is greater, that lye vnder the Command of a Solemne Vow; but for as much as all are obliged to walke in the wayes of virtue, and it is not lawfull to ſtop, til we arriue to the higheſt point, therefore to Perfection all are bound. And becauſe Perfection can not be attained, without fit meanes; and a prudent choiſe is requiſite in this regard: therefore, albeit None, of *Neceſsitie*, yet in *Congruitte*, All are bound, to make ſuch election as may moſt readily conduct them to that Noble end wherunto they aſpire. It is no diſparagement to other Religious Foundreſſes, or the deuout and zealous followers of their holy Inſtitutes, to affirme, that (herein) B. *S. Ciare* hath ſurpaſſed them all: and in Her, (though a wonder of women) it is leſſe admirable, yf we recount from whom she receiued Her Forme of Liuing. For as that great Deliuerer of the Law of Nature, hauing held fourtie dayes conference with God in *Mount Sinai*, was priuiledged from erring in his directions to the People, ſo long as he hept him to the *patterne that was shewed him in the Mount*: ſo that greater *Patriarck S. Francis*, after fourtie dayes familiar entercourſe with the World's Redeemer, in *Mont-Aluerne*, hauing receiued a better Law, a *Rule* of higher perfection, and deſcending from the Mount (not only with glory in his face, but the ſacred Wounds of our Sauiours dread Paſſion in his hands, feet and ſide) deliuered to his Brethren and followers to the World's end, the ſublime

Exod.25

Inſtitute

Inftitute of *Euangelicall pouertie*: and according to this *Patterne*, and by aduife of this
Vnerring Directour, *B. S. Clare* began Her Order, which hath fince beene propagated as
farre as the World is Chriftned It is this tranf-
cendent *Pouertie* (courteous Reader) this perfect abdication of all manner of proprietie, not
only in proper (which other Religious Orders haue) but in common alfo (the diftinctiue
cognifance of S. *Francis* children) which I haue
to commend to Thee, as the moft compédious
way to perfection heer, and immortalitie hereafter. Is it not a wonder, that this Angelicall
Virgin, hauing caft away all care of temporall
things, fhould be in continuall care, how fhe
might leaue this *Patrimonie* to her children,
that they might enioy *Nothing* ; making this
Her inftant Suite to the See Apoftolique, and
greatly exulting, when fhe had gained this
Priuiledge? And yet they will ceafe to wonder,
that confider, what extraordinary *priuiledges*
this facred *Pouerty* hath annexed to it. There
would be no end in reciting the many Elogies
giuen by pious and deuout Perfons to this
Soueraigne Lady, this *Euangelicall pouerty* : but
let it not feeme tedious that I recount fome of
Her *Prerogatiues*, confirmed to Her by *Patent*
of holy writ.

1. Art thou Poore? then thou art *Rich*. A Pa-
radoxe, you fay. 'Tis eafily proued *Pouertie* is
the *Riches* which purchafeth Heauen. *The Hun-
gry* (the poore) *he hath filled with good things,*

E   *and*

Luc.x. and the Rich he hath sent away empty.

2. Art thou Poore? by relinquishing all. *Not only in preparation of mynd, but also effectually for the loue of God.* It is an Argument of thy perfection, *If Thou wilt be perfect goe and sell all &c.* Matth.19.

3. Art thou Poore? thy prayers haue ready accesse and present speed at the Throne of Grace. *The poore man hath cried and our Lord hath heard him.*

4. Art thou Foore? Thou shalt obtaine pardon and mercy at God's hand. *He will spare the poore and the needy,*

5. Art thou Poore? Thou art highly dignified and ennobled. *Their name shalbe honorable before*
Psal.71 *him* To which sense our B. Sauiour spake, when hauing giuen S. Peter his reward of pouertie Matth.19. he addeth: *and many shalbe first, that are last, and last* (that is, in celestiall renowne) *that are first* (to wit here in temporall riches and dignities.)

6. Art thou Poore? Thou shalt be filled with all manner of comfort. *Thou hast prepared in thy sweetnes for the Poore of God.*

7. Art thou Poore? Thou shalt be protected from violence; and they shalbe smitten that offer iniury to thee. *Doe not violence to the poore,*
Psal.33. *neither oppresse the needy in the gate, because our Lord will iudge his cause, and will pierce them that haue pierced his soule.* And, *He shall saue*
Prou.22 *the children of the Poore, and humble the calum-*
Psal,71 *niator.*

8, Art

8. Art thou *Poore?* Then art thou like to Christ, who (as witnesseth the Apostle) *for you was made* poore, *whereas he was* rich, *that by his* pouertie, *you might* be rich. And, heare Christ himselfe: *Vnles euery one of you renounceth all that he possesseth he can not be my disciple.* Luc. 14.   2. Cor. 8

9. Art thou *Poore?* Thou hast gained a hauen of securitie; thou art freed from cares in the house, and impediments in the way. When K. *Ioachim* was led into Captiuity, all the Princes and Noblemen were caryed away also, *and nothing was left* (sayth the Scripture) *saue the* poore *sort of the People of the Land.*   4. Reg. 24.

10. Art thou *Poore?* Thou art freed from that Curse · *Woe vnto you that are Rich, for you haue your consolation.*

11. Art thou *Poore?* God will himselfe be solicitous of thee, & will inspire others to releeue thee, to their vnspeakable benefit. *But I am a begger and* poore: *our Lord is carefull of me.* psalm. 39. (a priuiledge which the Royall Prophet calleth *memoriam mirabilium:* psalm. 110.) And, *Blessed is the man that vnderstandeth concerning the needy and the* poore: *in the Euill day our Lord will deliuer him* Psal. 40. whence *Tobit* animateth his Sonne: saying, *Thou dost treasure vp to thy selfe a good reward in the day of necessitie: because Almes deliuereth from all sinne and from Death, and will not suffer the soule to goe into Darknes.* Chap. 4.   Pſ. 39.

12. Art thou *Poore?* Thou shalt assuredly attaine *Saluation,* and yf by a perfit renunciation

of All, the prerogatiue of eminent glory. And *euery one that hath left house or brethren &c for my Names sake, shall receiue an hundred fold and shall possesse life euerlasting.* Matth :19. and *you shall* (vers. precedent) *sit vpon twelue seates iudging the twelue Tribes of Israel.*

Nay, theirs is the kingdome of Heauen. Matt. 5. *Blessed are Poore for theirs is the kingdome of Heauen.* Ponder the word, *is*: He speaketh not in the *Future* , as in the other beatitudes. Whence S. Bernard. *What a strong wing is Pouertie,* wherby we haue a sudden flight to Heauen? For in the other virtues which follow, the promise runnes in the future tense: but to Pouertie *it is rather giuen than* promised, whence it is said in the present tense, because theirs is the kingdome of Heauen: but in the rest, they shall *inherit: they* shall be comforted: they shall possesse, &c. So He.

Loe heer the *Parsimonie* of the Poore: *twelue* Honours or *Priuiledges:* an ample prouision. So well assured , that you may call them the *twelue* Articles of the Poore mans Cred: rather, *Symbolum Apostolorum,* the *Badge* and cognisance of the *Apostles:* the contents of their *Obedience* , when they were dismissed by their grand Maister and Superior, on their Embassie to all quarters of the World. *Possesse neither Siluer nor gold nor mony in your purse , neither a wallet nor staffe nor shoes to your feet.* &c. Hence it is that our Holy Mother the Church hath graced the *Institute* of the *Seraphicall Father,* with the Title of *Apostolicall,* calling their manner of

Liuing,

Liuing, the *Rule of most eminent perfection*, and their *Pouertie, Euangelicall*, that tread in the steps of holy S. *Francis*, so neerly assimilating them to Christ and his Apostles, that no Rank of poore, Religious or others, can so iustly claime to that high priuiledge, the greatest of those formerly recited.

Now Beloued yf this discourse haue giuen thee any rellish of the way of Perfection, attend to thy Vocation. Thou wantest not glorious Precedents to set before thee. Consider Him, who (as yf Earth afforded something more precious than Heauen) came to seek Pouerty heer, which there was not to be found. Whence S. Bernard, sweetly: *Pouertie could not be found in Heauen. Now on earth was abundance of this kind, and man knew not the worth of it. Our Lord (therfore) the Sonne of God, enamoured on this Pouertie, descended from Heauen, to Espouse Her to himselfe, and by the account which he held of Her, to make her deare and amiable to vs also.* (O worthy of worthies which the world sets so litle by and is not worthy of!) And be secure, that this thy Christian fortitude shall be gloriously crowned. For yf his *Pouertie* made vs *Rich* (as testifieth the Apostle) what shall his *Riches* doe? Doubtles, He that was *Rich* with his Father, but *poore* with vs, *Rich* in Heauen, but *poore* on Earth, a *Rich* God, but a *poore* man: shall soone change our *Pouertie* into *Riches*, our Sack-cloth into Stoles of immortalitie, our teares into ioy and exultation, our momentanie suffering into

Bliſſe World without end.

There occurreth now to aduertiſe thee of
ſome things before I take my penne from the
paper: firſt that there are ſome ſworne enemies
(howſoeuer they diſguiſe themſelues) of
Poore Religious; that can not endure to ſee
them meritoriouſly exerciſe their humble pro-
feſſion euen to begge only that which is necef-
ſary for clothing and foode to ſuſtaine life in
the ſeruice of God, as though this, were to
ſeeke after riches, to heape vp treaſures & the
like: which Religious no leſſe abhorre & contemne then they maliciouſly impoſe vpõ them,
to impaire their Credits vitiating according
to their vſuall manner that which is truly laudable: to whom appertaineth thoſe words of
S. Baſile Conſt Mon. c. 7. That ſuch ſeculars
hath he knowes not what ſtrange conceit of
Religious as if togeather with there ſtate
they had preſently changed their nature, and
were not men, but of ſome other farre different mold: and conſequently they wrong the
ſeruants of God, & think ſometimes, that they
muſt ſcarce eate meate, as if they were not
made of fleſh and bloud: and if they ſee anie
of them attend to the neceſſities of their bodie,
they load them with reproaches and ſlanders,
and turning their calumniations from one vpon all the reſt, they cal them all gluttons and
bellie-Gods, & think not how themſelues doe
dayly feaſt it, and though they eate often in a
day, and cram themſelues with a great deale of

fleſh

flesh meate, & powre downe wine by whole
bowle-fuls, yet they gape after meate, as dogs
that are let loosse out of their chayne half-
starued. Thus speaketh *S. Basil* in defence of
Religious people.

Seeondly I trust that as the desire of aduan-
cing thy spirituall profite made me vndertake this *Translation* (which is totally out of the
R. F. Francis Hendriquez excepting the chapter inserted after the seconde: which is partly out of the History of the three and twenty
Protomartyrs of Iaponia, and partly also to wit
from **46**. page out of a certaine description of
S. Francis Order made by a Religious Priest at
the instace of a great deuote therof by occasion
of some detractios, for which reason I permitte
the author to vse his owne phrase against his
aduersary, though other times I reduce things
to the preset publishig of this life in mineowne)
so thou wilt be pleased of thy curtesy to corre-
cte patiently, & couer charitably the faults esca-
ped both in the print and English. Thus wi-
shing thee (deare Reader) by the perusall of
this little volume all surtherance in virtue, either by admiring Gods goodnesse and power
in his Saints in whom he is *Admirable*, or
by reducing to practize that which with proportion sutes with thy sexe or state: mind-
full of that of Sainct Austen : *That the
Examples of the Iuste are not proposed to our
View that wee should be iustified by them,
but that by imitation of them wee may likewise*

merite

To the Reader.

merite to be iustified by their Iustifier. I will
surcease to detaine you any longer.

ADIEV.

THE HISTORY
OF THE ANGELICALL VIRGIN
GLORIOVS Ste. CLARE,
MATCHLESSE PATTERNE
OF RELIGIOVS DISCIPLINE.
AND FOVNDRESSE
OF THE POORE DAMES
VVLGARLY STYLED THE POORE CLARES.

How ʃaint Francis repaires three Churches.

CHAP. I.

THe glorious and Seraphicall Father *S. Francis* moſt valourous and thrice renowned Captaine & Renewer of the Apoſtolicall Order of the poore Mendicants in the beginning of his Conuerſion, going forth of the City of *Aʃʃiſium* with intent to ſeeke out ſome

S. Bonauent. in the life of ʃaint Fran. c. 2

A ſolitarie

§.2.
Chron.1
p.ß.1.
cb.3.

solitarie retirement : there to apply himselfe
vnto mentall prayer , he passed neare vnto a
Church of S. *Damian* which for the great Antiquity was neare an vtter ruine and decay; the
Saint moued by the holy Ghost entred therin,
and falling on his knees, before the Image of
the *Crucifix*, he founde his soule replenished
with admirable consolation; when full repleat
with ardent feruour, hee presented and tendred
three seuerall times, at the throne of the diuine
Maiestie this humble supplication. O *high and*

A de-
uout
prayer
of saint
Francis.

glorious God Iesus Christ *Redeemer of the world,*
illuminate the darknesse of my heart and endow me
with true faith, constant hope perfect and inflamed
Charity, and the knowledge of thee my God: so as
I may euer accomplish thy diuine will and pleasure.
Amen Then holding his eyes fixed on this diuine Obiect and tree of life the *Crosse*, he po-
wred forth sho wers of teares and sent

The
Crucifix
speakes
to saint
Francis.

forth a million of sighes; and behold he heard a
voice proceeding from the *Crucifix* directed
to him saying three seuerall tims, *Francis ! goe*
and repaire my house, which as thou seest is ready to
fall: this maruellous voice did much amaze
him, there being not any in the Church but
himselfe , wherfore astonished and ressenting
the force and efficacie of these wordes , he
fainted , but in fine, returning to himselfe,
without delay he prepares to obey, & fortwith
vndertakes and attempts to repaire the materiall place wherin he had made his prayer: not
yet vnderstanding how the mysticall sence of
these words of God, intended the Restaura-

tion of an other Church, Redeemed by his pretious blond, as the vnction of the *Holy Ghost* did afterwards instruct him; which since he declared to his Religious: the same was by diuine Reuelation made manifest to the Vicar of *Christ* who was *Innocent* the third then sitting in the chaire of *S. Peeter*; who retiring ouer night to his chamber, with his thoughts ouerwhelmed with a pensiue care; pondering the calamities wherwith the Church was assaulted ther was in his sleep presented before him the Church of *S. Iohn Leteran* ready to fall to the ground, but a poore, abiect and contemtible man, of meane Condition coming stayed the falling therof, sustaining and vpholding it, with his shoulders: the next day behold the humble *Francis* with his Brethren came and prostrated themselues at the feete of his Holines: clothed in poore and patcht garments, tendering a new & vnaccustomed *Rule*, humbly petitionating him to approue the same: the Pope beholding the seruant of God, and obserueing the integritie, puritie, and innocencie of his soule conioyned with an admirable Contempt of the world demaunding the obseruation of Euangelicall *Pouertie* with a Seraphicall feruent zeale of the saluation of soules, sayd within himselfe; truly this is the man I haue seene, who shall help to supporte the Church of God, by his workes, words, examples, and doctrine, this vision manifested the qualitie, vocation, and life of *saint Francis* and his Order;

which

S. Bonau c. 3 §. 2. Luc. *Wad. ad annum. 1210. §. 13.*

A vision of Pope Innocēt the third

S. Francis demandes the confir mation of his Rule.

which should vphold the Catholick Church, and stay the falling therof, the which he atchieued in his life time, and after him his children became the supporting pillers therof. *Salomon* doth impart vnto vs a Reuelation he had in his life, which is a true symbole hereof, if not the same: I *haue seene* saith he *a Citie besieged on all sides and reduced to so great extremity that nothing was expected but vtter destruction, now being in this affliction, not able to withstand their Enemies, when behold there wa a man, founde in the Citie, who was poore and despised of all but must by himselfe: this man not withstanding poore and contemtible, was most wise and dexterous, & by his prudent aduise and counseile they founde the way to defeat the force of their Enemies, freeing the Citie from danger and setting it in all freedome and securitie.* What could haue bene more properly sayd for the glorious Patriarke S. *Francis* who like an other *Atlas*, doth support the two Poles of Christianitie. The Church in his time was *Assaulted*, lamentably torne and decayed with horrible scismes: the Romane Empire was rent with dissentioon and diuisions: *Constantinople* with all *Greece* had reuolted from the Obediéce of the soouueraine Bishop, the Citie of *Hierusalé* & all the *holy Hand* was giué in Prey to the *Sarazins* and Infidels; throughout all *Spaine* the Iewes and Barbarians did publickly in their Synagogues blaspheme the name of *Iesus Christ.* ouer all the Vniuers the Diuell tiranized by his adherents broching dis-

Ecclesiastes ca. 9

Bessoin a Sermon of S. Francis.

The troubles of the Church in saint Francis his time.

sentions Heresies and execrable vices: which now assembled like a squadron, menaced a totall subuersion: the Alarum was sounded through the whole Catholicke Monarchie: but none knew how to apply the remedy and redresse so great mischeifes and disasters: when most fortunatly there was founde in the same place the humble *Francis* a man abiect, and simple, little regarded of the world: making profession of *Pouerty*: but in the eyes of God most wise, prudent, and holy, who by his wisdome hath taught others the way how to appease & allay those tempestous billowes and repulse those hostile insurrections to preserue the Church, and exempt it from so imminent perils restoring peace to the world, together with deuotion, Euangelicall libertie, and Religious securitie, and after his example, a multitude haue enroled and registred themselues, vnder the Ensignes of this soueraigne, Apostolicall and holy *Pouerty*, recluding themselues into monasterie, arming themselues with virtue and learning, to repaire the breaches & ruines of the temple of God: reducing all to the Obedience of the Catholick Church, and laboureing in a most meritorious and edifying penitentiall life, to worke the saluatiõ of their neighbours, by preachings and good example. Goe ther *Francis* and repaire my house. This poore seruant of God, better grounded in humility and contempt of himselfe: returned to *Assisium*, where receiuing many affronts and

Luc.
Wadd.
Appar.
1. § 5 6
7.

S. Francis doth repare the ruin of the Church.

Chron.p.
B.1.c.6.
Luc.
Wadd.
appar.5.
§.8.13.
16.

iniuries, both from his parents and others, he began now to begge in the sight of those who before had seene him rich and opulent: and this obediently to execute what the diuine Oracle intimated vnto him, in the Church of *S. Damian*: bearing stones and other materialls on his shoulders, and so he repaired it by the helpe of the Almes & charitable beneuolence, which many moued by his vnwearied diligence and example, gaue vnto him. The like he performed in another Church of the B. Apostle *S. Peter*, to whom he was singularly deuoted, from thence he withdrew him selfe a quarter of a mile distant from *Assisium*. to a place called *Portiuncula* where there was an ancient Church of our B. Lady all ruinated, otherwise entituled *Saint Marie of Angells*, (where conformable to the name were knowne to haue often bene many Angelicall apparitions and visions) through the deuotion he bore to the Angells, & especially to the Queene of Angells he laboured much in the reparation thereof, yea he made a holy resolution to establish there his dwelling, in such forts as afterwardes it became the mother Church of the whole broadspreading and dilated Order of the *Freer Minors*. being giuen vnto him by an Abbot of *saint Benedicts* Order with consent of all his Religious. Aand notwithstanding that the sayd sayd Prelate with his Religious had made him an intire donation of the said place without any obligation: neuertherles *saint Francis* as a

S. Frāc.
repaires
three
Church

Portiun
cula is
the Mo-
ther
Church
of the
Order of
the Freer
Minors.

louer

louer of Euangelicall *Pouertie* and a wife and
prudent founder, defiring to poffeffe nothing
with propriety and dominion in this world:
but to enioy the bare vfe of things: prefented
euery yeare a Pannier full of little fish, which
he tooke in a Riuer hard by : in token of ac-
knowledgment: which the fayd Abbott, and
Religious accepted, with great reuerence and
deuotion : and in exchange gaue vnto him a
veffell of Oyle.

According to the opinion of the Seraphicall
Doctor S. Bonauenture by the three voyces
darted from the Crucifix at *Saint Damians*:
and the three materiall temples, which he hath
rapeired: we may vnderftand the three Orders,
which he hath founded and eftablifhed in the
militant Church : to withdraw many foules
forth of the miferable bondage of the tirant of
hell to beget and confecrate them to *Iefus*
Chrift.

*Of the inſtitution of the
order of the Freer
Minors.*

CHAP. II.

THis new Champion of *Ieſus Chriſt*, *Francis* like a terreſtriall Angell, or a Celeſtiall man: ſpent whole nights and dayes in prayer, in the Church of our *Ladies of Angels* beſeeching her, with teares and vnſpeaakble groanes, to be his Aduocate, and mediatrix with God: his prayers were ſo forceable, that by the merits and interceſſion of the ſacred Virgin, he was found worthy to conceiue and produce the ſpirit of truth, and Euangelicall *Pouerty*: for vpon one of the Apoſtles dayes being very attentiue at maſſe: as they read the Ghoſpell, wherin our Redeemer Ieſus *Chriſt*, preſcribing the forme of the Apoſtolicall life, when he ſent them ouer the world, to preach, ſaying, carry with you neither gold, nor ſiluer, purſe, nor wallet, nor two coats nor ſtaffe nor ſhooes, the ſaint illuminated with diuine illuſtration, cryed out with a ioy more then naturall:this is that which I ſeeke, this is

that

that which the very marrow of my soule doth desire: and presently putting of his shooes. casting away his stafe and wallet, he threw away the money, which was left of the Almes, as a thing most detestable, satisfying himselfe, with one habit, laying away his leather belt, he made vse of a grosse cord, beginning to lead an Apostolicall life in imitation of the words which in the Ghospell had bene spoken vnto him, as if an Angel had brought them from heauen: this was the yeare of our Redemption one thousand two hundred and eight, in the moneth of *October* vpon the day of S. *Luke*, S. *Francis* being then 27. years of age, two yeares being expired since his conuersion: the 12. yeare of the Popedome of Innocent the third.

In this kind of habit, this generous Captaine like an other *Seraphin* come frō the East, purifyed with the fyrie coale, kindled and inflamed with heauenly Charity: bgan to preach voluntarie *Pouerty*, Continencie, and Charity, true Pietye, and Pennance, the secure path to saluation: with simple yet forceable, graue, and seuere words which penetrated the hearts of the Auditors conuerting many sinners vnto God, teaching them the contempt & forsaking of riches, to fly vanities, the detestation of pleasures and delights, hairecloth and disciplines, lying on the ground, mortifying the flesh, passing whole nights in prayer, seruing God in feruour & deuotion, so as in short space he

Luc.
Wad. ad
annum.
1208.§
1.2.

became the Father of many children: who followed and imitated his example, drawne by the sweet Odour of his superemient virtues. The great increase of his Order may easily be collected, by the great number of Religious men assembled at the generall Chapter which *S. Francis* held at *Portiuncula* the yeare 1219. eleauen yeares after the institution of his Order, wherat his sincere and cordiall friend *S. Dominike*, founder of an other florishing Order in Gods Church would assist, with seauen of his Religious, there was numbred more then 5000 Brothers not counting thoe absent who stayed in the Conuent, to execute the ordinarie functions: and this by the assertion of *S. Bonauenture*: In the same chapter was receiued aboue fiue hundred Nouices.

This Order hath since, so multiplyed and increased, peopling the foure corners of the world: the rising of the Sunne, hath imbraced them with her refulgent Rayes: the west hath intertained them the north hath receiued thē: and the South hath afforded them mansions: there, is no corner in this Vniuers, where this holy Order hath not established monasteries, and the renowne of this great founder penetrated throughout al the Clymates of the earth: how many great Saints haue florished in this holy Order who are now inthroned in heauē: how many glorious and tryumphant Martirs, haue bathed and watered the earth with their bloud: both by Saracyns, Moores,

Chron.
p. 1. B. 1.
ch. 6

S. Bonauent. c. §.
10.

Henr.
Sedul.
in vit. S.
Francisci c. 3.

and

and Heretickes, how many learned Doctors,
darting euery where the refulgēt raies of their
admirable doctrine, by their voyce and penne
confuting Hereticks, confirming the faithfull in
the faith, and conuincing the obstinate impeni-
tence of sinners. How many illustrious presons
in his Order, haue bene raised to the dignity of Ecclesiasticall Prelacie: euen to the souueraigne dignity of Papacy.

Consider good Reader how the house of
God hath bene vpheld and repaired, according
to the commaundement of the *Crucifix*, by the
infatigable labours of his Ensigne-bearer humble *Francis* all ouer the world: or to cultiuate
the fertile fieldes of the Church: freeing soules
from the detestable seruitude of the Diuel,
consecrating them to the seruice of our great
God. If thou desire to know the effects this
fructifying vine hath produced foure hundred
yeares since; and to consider the worthy men
of this Order, the authours here cited will satisfy thy pious curiosity. See Henr. Seoul. in
c. 3. vit. S. *Francisci.* Luc. Wad. in his Annals.
Hieron. Plat. c. 30. 32. Gonsaga in Histo. Seraph.

But foras much as the prementioned Authors are not commonly at euery ones hand, as
being written in other languages: and to the
end it may more manifestly appeare, how deseruedly the style of the *Repairer* of Christs
Church is agreeable and due to the Great seruant of God holy S. *Francis*, whom it pleased

S. Fran-
cis the
Renew-
er of
Christ,
and the
Aposto-
licall life

B. Sauiour to ennoble and make remarkable
by the singular priuiledged Impression of his
sacred woundes, the signes of our Redemption,
the better to renew by him and his Order the
memory of his souueraigne Passion, almost
then extinguished in the hearts of Christians,
and restore againe the Apostolicall life and
discipline then depraued, and as it were abo-
lished and decayed: all which doth not a little
redounde to the honor of the Angelicall Virgin S. *Clare* to haue receiued hir Institution &
Rule of Religious life from so Grande and
highly dignifyed a Patriarck as was *S. Francis*:
I haue thought good here for the better satisfi-
ing the curiosity and deuotion of the Pious
Reader to insert in a distinct charecter the first
chapt. which the author of the History of the
3. & 20. 1. Martyrs of the Order beatifyed by the
Pope Vrban the VIII. with 3. of the societie of
Iesus, all crucified in Iaponia, which the Author I say of that History (printed at Doway)
prefixed to his worke, in regard, it doth breifly
and compendiously record and point out some
of the most memorable and Apostolicall acts of
his Order, & chiefly those enacted in these latter ages in both the East and West Indies.
Wherin the Freer Minors before all other
Religious haue that preheminency of glory to
be inuested with the titles of their first Apostles, as will most euidently be manifested by
the testimony of Hieronimus Platus the Iesuite in the ensuing chapter which foloweth

Of

❖❖❖❖❖❖❖ ❖❖❖❖❖❖❖❖❖❖❖❖❖❖❖❖❖❖❖

OF MANY AND ADMIRABLE ACTS
wrought by the holy Order of S. Francis in
the Church of God. But more especially in
these latter ages, in the Indies.

THE Seraphicall Father S. *Francis* sent by
Almightie God to repaire, vphold, and
propagate the holy Catholike Church
(as was reuealed in a vision to Pope Innocent
the third) not contenting himselfe to haue in
his owne person crossed the surging and peril-
ous seas, and trauelled ouer many barbarous and
Pagá Countries, to quench the heate of his ancient zeale and there to plant and erect the
triumphát standard of the holy Crosse where
of in himselfe he bore the liuing Image, but
euen after his death, he left to his children and
followers, as their filiall patrimonie the like
holy desires, which since his decease hoth so
enflamed their heroicke hearts, as that therein
they haue carried both fire and flames, to illuminate, heate, and reforme the most blinde,
colde, and schifmaticall nations of the spacious
world. I should digresse from my purpose of
being compendious, if I should any lóger lodge
my pen in these particularities: But in a word,
all Italie will testifie the truth hereof, by their
great and famous *Saincts, Antonie* and Bernar-

C   dine,

S Bon.
in V. S. F

S. Bon. in
vit. S. F.

dine, who by the maruellous effects of their
diuine doctrine haue drawne so many soules
out of the dangerous gulfe of this miserable
world, as that Italie seemed to liue onely by
their wholsome documents; they being constrained to preach out of Churches, in the publicke places and fieles by reason of the innume
rable multitudes of assembled people, who
were taken by the nets of these their pious
predications.

One onely Father of these; to wit. *S. Iohn
Capistran*, at a certaine time casting his nets
into the sea of Germany drew vp at one
draught, aboue twelue thousand soules, who
were sunke in sinne, and fallen from the faith of
our Sauiour Iesus Christ: and moreouer he
caused in that Countries such a reuolt from all
kinde of pride and vanitie that they brought
into the opē market places, whole Carts full of
fantastical headgeares, perewigs, bracelets
chaines, and the like to be all burned and con-
sumed by fire, in his presence.

Shall I goe into Greece to view the memorable
acts of *Hieronymus Ejaculansus*, who for the
like merits, was aduanced to the Papacie, and
afterward called *Nicholas* the fourth, whose
life and industrie brought backe by the hand of
his pious clemencie the Emperour and schis-
maticall Empire into the lap and bosome of
the Church of Christ.

I slip ouer in silence the heroicall acts of Brother *Iohn of Montis* with his companions, among

*Platus
l. 2. c. 32.*

*Pet. Rod.
l. 1. hist.
Serap &
Chr. F. M.*

*Sedul.
rom. ad.
vit. S. Fr.
c. 8.*

*Pet. Ro-
dulp. c. 7.*

the

the Tartarians, where they built diuers religious Conuents, in the yeare 1245.

As also the honours due to F. *Albert of Sartiano*, who like a swift and speedie cloud, did in an instant, so fertily water with his holy predications the thornes of Infidelitie, that from thence in a very short space budded the ruddie roses of holy Christianitie throughout all the Orientall parts; causing Conuents to be builded in Candia, Constantioople, Ierusalem, Syria, Greece, Ægipt, it with such fruit and promptitude, that he seemed to haue stoelen the wings and naturall prey of the soaring Eagle, by assembling on such a sudden so worthie a companie of constant Christians, and reducing of all Armenia to the obedience of the Church.

Sedul. cit.

Let vs now take a view of the Meridian Prouinces, and visit that industrious Gardiner B. O*dorie*, who merited to raise a dead man to life againe, out of an extraordinarie desire he had to baptize him, and did moreouer, so dexterously sow, plant, cultiuate, and water about the number of twentie thousand new plants of Christ, in a very short space, that they now in forme of their lillies of virginitie, in figure of the rose of martyrdome, and in fashion of the palmes of Iustice, serue him now for a Laurell of renoune and garland of glorie.

Pet. Ro-dulp. cit.

Platus l. 2.

Let vs rest our selues a while in Spaine, Catalognia, and Sardagnia, there to admire, in a time so impious and peruerse, that diuine and

Genz. p. 4°

wonderfull Freer Minor B. Saluator de Horta,
who caused the people of those places to hasten
to confession by thousands, as well by the efficacie of his speeches, as example of his ver-
tuous and holy life: And as for wonderfull miracles, we doe not reade that the Apostles, S.
Francis, or Iesus Christ himselfe did euer
worke so many (although he could haue done
farre more, and greater, if he had pleased, *Ma-*
iora horum: faciem) for there was presented to
Pope Paul the fift, fifteene thousand, one
hundred, seauentie and eight, all passed through
the hands of publicke Notaries; not counting
twise as many others of lesser moment: He
dyed kising the Crosse, the yeare 1564. and
his holy body remaineth yet to this day both
entire and maniable.

Let vs now saile into Affrica, and there cõ-
sider King Curo, much busied in soliciting the
King of Spaine, about earnest affaires, sending
to this effect, for Embassadour, the R. F. Francis Zirano, of this Seraphicall Order, the yeare
1603. who, in a word, being apprehended by
the bloud-sucking Moores of Algiers, was
sentenced to be flayed aliue, and afterwards
burned. O what barbarious crueltie is this, on
the one side, and what admirable constancie,
on the other! Behold foure bloudy Execu-
tioners, with sparckling eyes, and foaming
mouthes, like rauening wolues, their sacrile-
gious armes lifted vp, with euery one his ra-
sour, ready to put their vniust offices in exe-

cution

Chron. F.
M. 10. 4.

cution, the first opens his skinne, fró the necke
downe all along his shoulders, and the others
drawing it in fashion of a Crosse, tares it
downe his body, and then all foure tooke him
by the hayre and eares, and cuts a greate Crosse
vpon his head, and then they flay most in-
humanly the sides, backe & forepart thereof: and afterwards with more then barbarous
crueltie, they flay his tender face in like man
ner. O blessed martyr, art thou not yet deade
Al as no, I heare thee still to sing; *Benedicite*
Spiritus & anima iustorum Domino, and make an
end wholly of this Canticle, before thou
rendrest thy life, whilest these wicked Mahumetans would make thee denie thy holy Faith,
vexing themselues to see that by how much
they rage and storme at thee, by so much the
more they heare the Eccho of thine vndaunted
constancie, to adde, *Sancta Maria, ora pro nobis*.
But peace a while O iust Abel, these impious
Cains haue yet their rasors to rip open the
most tender part of thy harmelesse body, to
wit the nauell: to which being come, these
bloudy Butchers exenterated him with such
force and violence, that he had but onely leasure enough to lift vp his eyes to heauen, and
say with a loud voice, *In manus tuas Domine,*
commendo spiritum meum: thus yeelding vp his
soule into the hands of his Creatour. But being
dead, the very winds ceased not to testifie his
innocencie with such strange and vnheard of
tumultuous tempests, that the cruell Moores

Psal.23.

C 3   thought

thought they should all haue beene slaine in
the place, so that they had not leasure to burne
or destroy his holy body.

P. Mart.

Let vs adioyne vnto those, the glorious Fa
ther F. Danan of Valencia in the same Affrica
the yeare 1533. where, for the onely faith of
Iesus Christ, he was cast into burning flames,
without receiuing any more hurt thereby then

Dan. 3.

Sydrach, Misech, and Abdenego; so that they
were forced at length to put him to death by
the stroke of the sword.

Iun.
Ad ann.
1615.

Let vs now hoyse vp saile to the vncouth
Ilands, (the holy Ghost will procure vs a wind)
to accompanie foure Freer Minors of France
the yeare 1615. who arriuing with the French
men in the Ile of Canada, celebrated there the
first Masse in the famous Citie of Quebec.

P. Mariã
l. 4. c. 28
Chron.
Bald.

But that which may as much moue vs as
the rest, are the heroicke deeds performed in
the Ile of Moluc, by two glittering starres of
the Order of Freer Minors, the one called F.
Sebastian, and the other B. Antonie: the first
preached there with such zeale and efficacie,
that he conuerted and baptized fiue great Po
tentates, and going farther into the Ile Taco
lande (subiect to the Mahumetans) after infi
nite labours, foũd there at length the Crowne
of Martyrdome by the sword: his poore body
being afterwards made a marke to shoote at in
the common place of exercise, where hauing
receiued a thousand shots of sharpe arrowes,
was afterward cast into the water, but could

neuer

neuer be made to finke. Meane while, his com
panion B. Antonie , being faire and young, *ibid.*
feemed fo beautifull in the eyes of the Kings
daughter, that fhee deferred his condemnation
with hopes to haue enioyed him as her huf-
band : What doth not Satan fuggeft to the
minds of loofe and lafciuious woemen, to alie-
nate a foule from her Creatour? But this
chaft Iofeph , left behinde him rather his
cloake , I meane his skinne then his vowed
Chaftitie. But this bloudy and rauenous fhee
woolfe , feeing her felfe mifprized by him,
commanded all her Ladies and Damfels to
take each of them a knife or punyard in their
hands and fo daunce all in a rounde , into the
middeft of which fhee caufed to be brought
this poore and innocent Religious, as naked as
he was brought into the world : O prodigie!
O crueltie! O vnheard of Martyrdome! The
one ftrikes the knife into his arme , the other
into his backe, another markes him on the face,
another on the head ,and fo finally by a ling-
ring and cruell death (by the hands of thefe
blouddy and tyrannicall woemen) was he
brought to his laft gafpe, where at length they
cut of his head like another S. Iohn, the great
precurfor of the Meffias: but with this admira-
tiō, that his head being put vpō the top of a lōg
poale, it fpake miraculoufly & preached of thofe
effeminate cruelties the fpace of two whole
dayes, as if it had beene aliue, although difioy-
ned frō its body. Haue you euer heard or feene

a more

Sap. 4.

a more rare and admirable thing? O *qaam pul-chra est casta generatio cum claritate! immortalis est memoria eius:* Speake, speake then, O how faire and glittering is the chast generation, its memorie liues now immortall in this great Martyr, who forsooke the nuptiall pleasures of impietie, to wed, himselfe in faith to his celestiall and dearest Espouse, called to the marriage of the lambe, to adhere æternally to his blisse and glorie.

S. Anton
34. tit.
24. p. 3.

Let the Bulgarians rise againe, and confesse that all their kingdome had beene lost, if (about the yeare 1366. the Freer Minors, had not brought it backe againe into the sheepe fold of the holy Church of God. Would you euer beleeue that in fistie dayes alone, they should (by the sound of eight Euangelicall trumpets onely) call into the lap of the Church more then two hundred thousand persons, and make them to surcease their rebellious insurrections against their king?

Plagus l.
2. de bon.
statu.
Franc.
recit.
Iouin.
Ester. hist
Mart.
Gorc.
Chroniq

I keepe you too long from arriuing into America, I leaue in Armenia Gonsales Saurata: among the Mides and Persians, Paschal & Gentil: S. Bonauenture in France, Blessed Pacificus, the Martyrs of Gorcome and diuers others in the low countries.

The aforementioned exploites may more then sufficiently suffice to confirme that the Seraphicall Father hath left in legacie, a rich inheritance of faithfull and magnanimous children to our holy mother the Church. Yet

a 1

all these couragious Captaine seeme to haue
done nothing in comparison of the admirable
fruit which others of the same order haue produced, as well in the Orientall as Occidentall
Indies, to the honour of God, and profit of
sundry Christian Princes, but especially to the
Catholike Maiestie of the King of Spaine: For
in the West Indies, neuer had he that found &
conquered it (to wit, Christopher Columba)
obtained the graunt of his request, no, not so
much as accesse to Ferdinand King of Sicilie,
had not the intercession of the Reu. Fa. Iohn
Piret bene interposed: yet for all that, ceased
not the Princes and Counsellers to laugh at
the hopes of Columba, seeing it was onely
grounded vpon the fauour of one poore Freer
Minor (as all Historians who write of the Indies haue recounted) notwithstanding, without which aduenture, and effect, what great
losse, and vnspeakable damage, had the kingdome of Spaine sustained: But what was the
recompence of these poore Fathers? Truly
none at all, but onely the honour to accompanie the said Generall, with his brethren, &
to enrich the holy Church as much with
soules, as Spaine with treasures: who before
had totally reiected the request of Columba,
for the space of seauen yeares, vntill these
Fathers tooke the matter in hand, and happily
obtayned it for him: who afterwards, as well
for this respect, as others, were chosen for the
vantgard of so generous a conquest, about

Cornil.
Ving.
Ant.
Mag.
Hist. v-
nia des
Indes c.
3.
Sedul.
comm.
vit. S.
Franc.
P. Ma-
rian.

the yeare 1493. where they behaued themselues
so religiously, as that in the yeare 1529. one of
these Brothers, called Br. Peter of Gaunt,
writing to the Fathers in the low Countries,
affirmed, that he alone, with his companion,
had then baptized two hundred thousand Infi
dels: and added farther; that they had at that
time about fiue hundred children vnder their
tuition, whom he had so instructed in the Ca
tholick faith, that he sent them euery Sunday
to catechise and preach in the villages, what
they had learned at home in the weeke-time:
And to this effect they went sometimes ten,
twentie, or thirtie miles to promulge the faith
of *Christ*: I leaue you to consider with what fruit
& profit: In so much as that about three yeares
after, the chiefe Bishop of one the principall
Cities of the new world Mexico, wrote vnto
their Generall, that he had catechized & bapti
zed, with the assistance of his religious Brethrē,
the true children of *S. Francis*, about ten
hundred thousand persons, and a few yeares
after, seauen millions, according to the report
of Surius: And all this is spoken but of the Ci
tie and kingdome of Mexico onely: a Citie
that Abraham Ortelius calls the Queene of
the world: And Sedulius, a faithfull Historio
grapher, sayes, it is gouerned by thirtie Poten
tates, who haue an hundred thousand men
vnder their charge and command, and f whom
very often, they sacrifice a thousand persons,
and euery yeare there are twentie thousand

Sedul.
cus. S ur.
ad ann.
1558.

hearts

hearts taken out of the bodies of little childrē, to be offered vnto the Deuils. For confirmation whereof, peruse the letters placed at the end of this treatise. O strange metamorphose ten, twentie, or thirtie yeares after, of a Citie, before abounding with vice and iniquitie. and of which one might iustly haue said that which S. Leo said of Rome: *Quæ erat discipula superstitionis, facta est magistra veritatis :* That which before was a disciple of new superstitions, is now made the mistrisse of truth and veritie, yea, an Academie of so many thousand conuertants to our holy Catholike Faith. O what an happie gleaming was there made in this holy haruest, by the labours of the poore Freer Minors ! Who being not able of themselues, by reason of their smal number, to serue so many soules, cryed out for succour, and yet, not till fortie yeares after, could they obtaine the least assistance wherein, vntill, the Dominicans, Augustins, Iesuites, and others, who haue also borne apart with them in these glorious conquests valiantly contriumphed with them ouer the rest. But aboue all, (after the holy Church) the King of Spaine, and Blessed house of Austria, haue alwayes entrusted the most important businesses to this Order of S. *Francis* sending them to the Indies, throughout all the 28. Kingdomes that are subiect and tributarie thereunto ; and likewise to the purchasing of other new found lands, sometimes as Embassadours, Inquisitors, Protectours, Bishops, and

Preachers, there to assure and enlarge his
crowne and Kingdome. And to goe no farther,
you haue seene it your selues in these your
present times, in the peace so important and
difficult, of France and Spaine, of Holland and
the low Countries, which these Fathers to wit
R. F. Bonau. a Calatagirone Generall of his
Order for Fraunce, and the R. F. Iohn Neyen
Comissary of his Order in the Low Coûtries,
haue bene sent to bring to effect and haue happily cōcluded: the benefit of which, as well Europe, as the East and West-Indies doe daily
experience. *O quam pulchra sunt pedes Euange-*
lizantium pacem!

Yes Occidentalls, you might haue remar-
ked in this Apostolica'l Freer Minor, & simple
Lay-Brother by profession, B. Peter of Gant,
who (besides al that I haue already spoken of
him) erected, himselfe alone, more then an
hundred Churchs in these westerne Indies. His
dexteritie in conuerting of soules was so great
(labouring therein the space of fiftie yeares)
that he had dispensation and graunt sent him
from the Pope, and Superiours of his Order to
be installed Archbishop of Mexico: But this
precious pearle, desired rather to liue still in
the shell of his holy humilitie, then to take
vpon him so great an Ecclesiasticall dignitie, to
the end, that he might thereby, to the greater
misprize of himselfe, the more freely labour
in the haruest of the vnmanured Indies, with
the R. F. Iohn Couureur, Guardian of Gant, &

B

B. Iohn de Aora, who were sent thether at the
very point of so difficult an assault, by Charles
the fift, the yeare 1523. These ensuing verses
were sent vnto B. Peter, into the Indies, by the
aforesaid Emperour Charles V.

Non valet absque Petro, Cæsar, cum Cæsare Petrus.
  Consolidat terris sceptra fidemque Deus!
Quam grandis Gaudis! quam candida lilia pandis,
  Horte voluptatis, vera cauerna Petri.
Quam magnus Petrus! Minor Atlas ille secundi
  Mundi simplicibus regna ferens humeris,
Quã magnus Carolus! quasi quinta potentia Regum
  Sed nisi cum Petro, non bene tantus erat.

Who's Charles the fift, if Peter's not his friend
  Combinde together to the farthest end
Of th' vtmost world, the Gospels rayes shall reach
  And with them Cæsars gouernement shall streach
O God! what good vnto the Gospell hath
  Bene got by this Apostle of thy Faith?
O Gand! what land hast thou thy Soueraigne gaind?
  In yeelding such a Columne, which sustain'd
Th' Antasticke worlds: Huge Axell, like t' another
  Atlas, though but the Minoritts Minor Brother:
In whom our Sauiours sacred words proou'd true
  He that is least shall be the great'st mongst you:
Cæsar was great, yet then this Cedar lesse
  Which did his realme enlarge, and Gods encrease.

This said Emperour Charles V. sent thither
also another firme Pillar of this new and mag-

nificent

nificent building, to wit, F. Iohn Lumaraga, of
this holy Order also, vnder the title of Prote
ctour Generall of the Indies, where he behaued himselfe so worthie his vocation, as
well in person of a Preacher, as in nature of an
Archbishop, that on a certaine time he wrote
into these Countries, that (besides what you
shall see in his letters adioyned to the end of
this Historie) he had baptized ten hundred
thousand persons, and broke in peeces more
then twentie thousand inchanted Idols. O vi
ctorious Dauid! who canst iustly boast to
haue ouercome more then ten thousand Phili
stins, by the onely word of thy pious predica
tions! O magnanimous Hercules, who by
the vertue of the Crosse, hast throwne downe
and destroyed so many monstrous Idols! O
inuincible Sampson, who by the power of the
Gospell (as by another iaw bone) hast ouer-
turned the enemies of the Faith and his Catho
licke Maiestie.

May you not then with very great reason
(deare Reader) say vnto Charles the fift, as S.
Leo said to the Citie of Rome: *Quamuis enim
multis aucta victorijs tu Imperij tui terra marique
protuleris, minus tamen est, quod tibi bellicus labor
subdidit, quam quod pax Christiana subiecit.* Know
mightie Charles, that although thou shouldest
incomparably haue enlarged thine Empire,
as well by sea, as by land, triumphing ouer ma
ny worthie and victorious nations, yet in the
end wouldest not thou finde, that all the la

bours of thy warlike souldiers haue euer
brought so many rebellions persons vnder the
obedience of thy scepter, as holy Ghristian
peace hath subdued in the barbarous Indies, by
the meanes of onely three poore and peaceable
Freer Minots (as are mentioned by diuers
Historiographers) to wit, B. Peter of Gant,
who (as aforesaid) with his companions conuerted two hundred thousand persons to the
Faith of Christ.

Two yeares after one of this order the R.F.B.
Martine de Valentia, with his companions
baptized twelue hundred thousand And at the
same time by the most R F.Iohn Lumazaga, of
this Order were also conuerted then hundred
thousand more. If any one call in question the
veritie hereof, let him reade the Workes of the
most illustrious and R. F Francis Gonzaguez,
Bishop of Mantua, the Annals of this Order
the letters from Iaponia, Sedulius. Surius,
Marianus, and diuers others, who will giue
him sufficient intelligence of the ineffable and
miraculous haruest reaped & procured by the
aforesaid holy Fathers, which was so much the
more easily effected, by how much they saw
these poore children of S. *Francis* to misprize
and contemne all humane commodities, and
confirme their speeches by working of miracles
and raising of the dead.

These great Apostles deserued that their victorious triumphs, should be seconded by
other, no lesse noble and valorous Captaines:

for not only the weft, but Eaft Indies alfo which were firft found out, and fubdued by that generous Colonell Vafco Gamas in the reigne of Emanuel king of Portugal; who tooke eight of thefe Fathers with him, to breake the yce of fo difficult and dangerous an enterprife but (by Gods affiftance) it prooued fo fauorable and fuccefsfull vnto them, that in the yeare 1500. they fewed their fertile graine in the kingdome of Calecut, and entred into Brafile, where the firft Maffe was fung the 24. of Aprill, the fame yeare 1500. In which Countrie were crowned three glorious Martyrs of this Order, whofe warme bloud did fo plentifully water this new vine of *Iefus Chrift*, that the totall narration therof is impoffible to be recounted. Iudge you of the plentie of the harueft by the number of the infatigable labourers of this Order, who where therein employed. The R. F. Platus à Iefuite doth nūber in thefe parts (to wit the Eafte Indians) thirteene Prouinces erected for the habitation of thefe Freers, fortie yeares before euer the Fathers of the *Societie* entred into thofe Indies. And you muft vnderftand, that by the name of Prouince, the Freer Minors meane a congregation of fo many Conuents vnder a Prouinciall fo that one Prouince of the Order dilates it felfe fometimes into fundry kingdomes, hauing it. 10. 30. and many times 60. Conuents each of them in their Dominions, and together with thofe of Religious woemen, fometimes

more

Hift.
Plat.

Hift.
vnia. l. 1
c. 19

Lib. 1. de
bon. Re-
lig. c. 30

more then an hundred: The Prouince alone
de Sancto Euangelio in the West Indies, containes more then 67. Conuents of men without mentioning those of woemen, as Clares
and those of men or wemen to wit, Tertiaries
of both of which, there are also in both
the Indies: From whence you may easily
gather, how much the Order of S. *Francis* fru-
ctifieth in those quarters, and how many faithfull labourers there are in those parts, whose
names to vs are not knowne, but it sufficeth
that they are written more particularly in the
booke of life.

I should fill whole volumes and reduce the
wide Ocean (as it were) into a shell, if I should
goe about to recount all their heroicall iacts,
performed for the aduancement of the Faith
of *Chrift*, and therevnto adioyne the names of
all those couragious and magnanimous souldiers, who as couragious as Iosua, feared not
first to enter vnto those barbarous Countries,
not yet gaue backe for all the cruelties of
those terrible Gyants, the inhabitants thereof,
plentifully, abounding in infidelitie, siluer, and
gold, that which these men (*Generatio quæren-
tium faciem Domini*) so much abhorred, but
persisted still couragious in abolishing their
impietie, rendering these impious Pagans cap-
tiues to the Faith of *Chrift*, and leading them in
triumph, like rebels, bound to the Chariot of
Christianitie, which carries them securely to
their immortall glorie: and this in so great a

S. Fran-
cis infti-
tuted 3.
Orders.

E number

Theat.
totius
orbis &
P. Marib
l.1.Chro.

number, as that all the triumphant Romanes haue not to shew so many trophees of their greatest victories, purchast by the bloud of so many thousand warlike souldiers, of their chiefest Colonels, who like vndaunted Lyons feared not boldly to present themselues before the Face of their deadliest enemies, as hath one ly twelue naked and peaceable lambes of this holy Order, vnder the conduct of that great

Sur. cit.
& Epist
eiusdem
Mart.

Duke, and poore Freer Minor, Martin de Valentia, sent into the West Indies the yeare 1524 arm'd onely with the armour of holy Obedience, and protected with the shield of the loue of God. There was not one amongst them al that wanted courage to quell the rage of those misbeleeuing Infidels, for they had all of them as speedie wings as inflamed zeale, in this their glorious enterprize, each of them hauing conuerted and baptized the yeare 1531 more then an hundred thousand Indians. In

Sedu. cit.

like manner, Charles the fifth sent from all his kingdomes (and also from these quarters, to wit, from Bruges and Gand) very frequently great multitudes of Freer Minors, the particularities of whose Apostolicall acts archieued in this holy mission, would be too tedious to recount.

Sur. cit.
& Se
dul. cit.

The aforesaid Charles the fift, acknowledging the honour due to the Order of *S. Francis*, did not onely send those of Bruges and Gand, as aforementioned, but in the yeare 1520. hauing discouered the East Indies also, contented

not

not himselfe onely there to haue erected certaine significatiue Pillars of his farther trophees, engrauing thereon, PLVS VLTRA, but also sent some of those Freers thither, for markes or Pillars, to signifie vnto the inhabitants thereof, that they were likewise to passe PLVS VLTRA, to wit, from their accursed infidelitie to the lauer of Christianitie, and from it to the conquest of the hauen of happinesse. Pillars truely, more shining then those which conducted Israel at midnight to the land Promise: For at the splendour of their doctrine both the king and kingdome of Mexicacan were conuerted to the Faith, the king calling himselfe Francis, in acknowledgement of the obligation which he had to the holy Order of S. *Francis*. F Iohn of Tapis, conuerted at the same time, the Quinquinists, and afterward, for his recompence, suffered a glorious Martyrdome.

Our intended breuitie in this holy Histories hath forced vs to let slip the particularities of the fortitude of F. Peter of Garobily, who spent diuers dayes in pulling downe of the prophane Idols, which were there so plentifully erected in euery place, that he brake and threw downe more then ten thousand euery day

Likewise we must leaue the founder of the Church of Peru and Brasile, called F. Iosse de Rijcke, bone at Mechline.

The yeare also 1530. B Ferdinand Bassachio

Chron. F
Min. t. 4

Epist.
fratris
Iodici.

Chron F
M.v.t.4

E 2

was the first that taught the Indians of Cantli. tanio to sing in the Church.

F. Mari.
Chron.l.
4.c.34.

I passe ouer the life of B. Alphonsus Ordonnez, who droue away the Deuills. And the merits of Br. Francis of the Crosse, at whose death the bells did ring of themselues, which miracle was cause of the conuersion of many Indians.

Gonz.
hist. Seraph.p.4
Gonz.
ibid.

I leaue likewise the particular fruite produced by the Embassie of the R.F. Lewis Portugais, sent by king Narsinga, to the Viceroy of the Indies: As also of F. Denis, martyred in the Prouince of Cumana.

Goz.p.3

And likewise it would be too tedious to report at large how many thousand misbeleeuers were conuerted by the feruent zeale and industrie of the R.F.B. Ximenes in new Spaine, refusing diuers Bishopricks, for the better opportunitie of preaching to the people.

In like manner, we say nothing of the predi cations and martyrdomes of those who con uerted the heresies of Scibola; nor of Br. Hyacinthus of *Saint Francis*, whose bodie was found whole and entire many yeares after his death.

Chron.
F. Min.

Nor of F. Iames of Denmarke, who being in the Indies, had the same day a reuelation of the death of Charles the fifth, and was the first that administred the holy Eucharist in Mexi ca came.

Gonz.p.
3.c11.

Blessed are they who saw, and considered the zeale and holy affections of F. Iohn of S.

Michael,

Michael, and those of the Reuerend Fathers
Angel of Valencia and Daniel of Italie, martyred in the Indies: and Antonie Maldonat, who
like another Alexis, left his kindred, and seauen
thousand fiue hundred crownes, in yearely re-
uenues, to goe, in nature of a poore Freer Minor to the Indies: where he might iustly say
with the king of Sodome, *Da mihi animas, cæ-
tera tolle tibi:* Giue me soules, & keepe all things
else vnto thy selfe. *Gen.14*

Let vs leaue the miraculous F. Alphonsus
in Peru, with F. Iohn of *S. Francis,* who being
in prayer, and vttering these Blessed words,
Deus meus, illuminatio mea, obtained, at the same
instant, the gift of the Mexican tongue, and
afterwards became very famous for destroy-
ing of the Idols, and recalling to the sheepfold
of *Christ* those deceiued soules who long had
gone astray in the fields of Infidelitie. *Chro. F.*
Min.t.4

Peter Bernard Cosin, assisted by the Omnipotent power, retorted back againe the arrowes which were shot at him; although afterwards he was gloriously martyred, the yeare
1555. *P. Mari.*
in Chro.
l.3,c.2.

F. Iohn of Sori, in the Citie of Chaul,
conserued the towne, being besieged and des-
parate, Almightie God hauing reuealed the victorie vnto him. *Ibid.*

F. Francis Colmenaria healed the Indians of their vlcers, by the onely sight of his
letters. *P. Ma-*
tian,cit,
l.2,

Peter Torobio Mutolinia, which signi- *Gonz.p.*
3.

fies

fies Poore in the Indian tongue, conuerted for
his part, more then foure hundred thousand
Indians.

Let vs now goe into China, and there re-
uiew a while, the zeale of the poore Discalsed
Freers F. Peter of Alpharo, F. Iohn Baptist, &
B. Francis Marian, for whose sake God did
seeme to haue blinded the Centinels and Gards
of the Sea ports of China, that those holy seruants of his might safely arriue to the Citie of
Canton, and afterwards to Machian, without
any molestation, against all vsuall custome, for
those places are ordinarily so strictly garded,
that they suffer no strangers whatsoeuer, to
enter there with such facilitie. Those industrious Apostles were of the Prouince of our
holy Martyrs (for whom we write this Historie) and for whose honour we haue here
adioyned their heroicall acts. But first before
their departure from the Philippines, they
there conuerted twice three hundred thousand Indians, and being enriched with so many
victorious spoyles, they thence tooke their
iourneyes into the Countries of China.

¶ Didacus and his Companions, would be
discontented if we should not remember them
in passing by the Canaries, where they were
the very first Preachers, and by words and miracles conuerted an infinite number of infidell
people in that suggered iland.

Whilest I runne ouer so many braue Apostles
of the Indies, I must make you smile at the

follie of the inhabitants of Cacaſtlane and A maxocotlane, who are accuſtomed to weare, as an ornament their beard, guildeth with gold, ſiluer or tinne: But that great Apoſtle R. F. Fracis Laurence a Freer of the Seraphicall Order made them at length ſo deteſt this fooliſh faſhion, as that they, with very great prompti, rude, cut of their beards, and caſt them into the fire, and of the metall which proceeded there of (according to the teſtimonie of Biſhop Gonzaguez) there were made ſeauenteene bells, the which weighed 141. pounds, and were afterwards put into the new Churchs. This generous ſouldier conuerted alſo the people and nations of Ortritcepa, Texogium, the Prouince called the Crowned Freers, Cacaſtlame, Baſcamenes, and Cacolatraces, in the viſit of which he was martyred with an yron barre, according as he before had prophecied. I leaue you to conclude how many people he conuerted, by the multitude of beards, frõ the which was taken as much metrel as made them ſeauenteene belles.

P. Mariana, cit.
It were impoſſible to recount all the heroicall acts which B. Martin of Ieſus performed in new Spaine.

Of Br. Iohn Calera in the kingdome of Calixco, where he ſuffered a glorious martyrdome.

P. Marian. cit. l. 3. c. 5.
Of Br. Anthonie of Colart in Diſtatanio, who was martyred by the Indians of Fagaloncis.

Of

Chron. F Min. t. 4

Of B. Iohn of Grenado Commiſſarie o new Spaine.

Of B. Luke of Amaldobar in Mexico, hauing the gift of curing diſeaſes.

Ibid.
Ibid.
Gonz. cit. p. 3.

Of B. Iohn Bournon in Mexico.

Of B. Francis Soto in Mexico, who generouſly refuſed the Arch-biſhoprike thereof.

Ibid.
Chron. 16
Chron.

Of B. Iohn Sëurade Preacher to the Quinqueniſts.

Of B Francis martyred in Moluca.

Of B. Iohn, martyred going by Sea to the Ile of Zelan.

Gonz. cit

Of B. Stephen, martyred by the Maluaries.

Chron. F Min. t. 4

Of B. Alphonſus Betanze, the firſt Apoſtle among the Caſtaricanes, who there baptized 4000. perſons.

Ibib.
Ibid.

B. Francis of Torrio, in Fucatanea.

B Rodericus Beneuento in the Prouince de Sancto Euangelio in Calixco, and the Vallie of Vandera.

B. Iohn Clauſe, in Pocye, martyred going to Xacatica: and a thouſand others, which I willingly leaue out, and wittingly forget rather then by prolixity become tedious or troubleſome vnto you.

Franc. Rediuiuus cit.

Gonſaguez, a moſt pious Generall of this holy Order, makes mention of many other effects, which want of time and oportunitie will not here permit me to rehearſe. But I can by no meanes ſuffer F. Iohn of Valeconte

to reſt in the ſad ſepulcher of darke obliuion,
who was ſent by the King of Portugal, (and
demanded by the King of Zelano) into the Indies, the yeare 1540 where for the conuerſion
of the King, he offered to caſt himſelfe into
flaming fire, or into a denne of moſt horrible
Serpents. His voyage was not in vaine, for
he there conuerted the King ſucceſſour to the
aforeſaid; the Queene his wife, the King of
Candie, and almoſt all the kingdome of Zelano.

I haue expreſſely reſerued for this place
the merits of B. Martin of Valentia, the which
exceed all narration, by reaſon of the greatneſſe
of his ardent zeale concerning the conuerſion
of the Indies, whither he went the yeare 1524.
and receiued from God two ſeuerall reuelatōs
of the Countrie of China, many yeares
before euer *S. Francis Xauerius* vndertooke that
voyage: His life was as admirable as his death
miraculous; for his body was found whole
and entire full thirtie yeares after his deceaſe;
and very ſhortly after they found nothing at all
in his ſhrine or coffin, no, not ſo much as his
duſt or aſhes; & who knowes whither Almightie God hath raiſed it againe, or tranſlated
or reſerued it for a more glorious ſhrine. His
worthie acts I will here recoūt in a few verſes
conformable to his name.

Sedu. cit P. Ma- rian.

Viuebat raptus Chriſto confixus amanti.

Vixit in hoc Chriſtus, non erat hoc quod erat

Talibus

Talibus emeruit magnus virtutibus orbes
Meritaquam fœlix vate valente vales!
In te pertrax.t tot milia, totq̃, phalanges,
Quot magnes æuum millia, nulla valet,
Quam validus valor hic! valet illa Valentia valde
Quam valuit validans Indica regna valens.

Grafted in Christ he liu'd, and Christ in him
  For he was not the Creature he did seem,
How puissant wer'st thou Mexico in this
  Thy powrefull Prophet? How great was thy blisse
Enioying him? Whose worth was such, that he.
  Deseru'd a Monarch in this world to be
If that a Load stone thy great'st Mountaine were,
  Yet could it not attract such store (if 't were
In possibilitie) of needles, as did he
  Millions of soules to Christianitie:
O more then human power Valencia thou
  For them in both the worlds art sainted now.

Vpon the same:

This holy Father, for his gifts diuine
  (Blest Martin) in our Hemisphere did shine
A glorious starre: till God, who did behold
  (In's mercie) th'Indias, which in darkenesse howl'd
Sent streight to dissipate their clowds, this Sunne
  Who first in Mexico his course begunne.
And there did set, yet first did worke so much,
  That th'Indian equaliz'd the Roman Church,
Whose feruent Zeale could not at all becoolde
  By frozen want, or miserie controlde,

No tyrannie could close vp his mellifluous lipps
  Nor interposing Barbarisme eclipse
His Faiths cleare beames. This glorious Palme the
  It was suppreft, the loftier did sore: (more
Or like a Torrent ftopt, the swifier ran
  Till he arriued in the Ocean
Of Gods large mercie, with the soules which he
  Embarked had for Chriftianitie
A wealthyer Carracke nere to th'Indies went
  Nor greater treasure since from thence was sent
For he enrich'd their Minds and Mines with Ore
  Which were but leade and Copper both before.

O wonderfull prouidence of Almightie God!
that this bright Sunne-beame Martin, should
be sent to illuminate a new world, Farre
greater then that which Martin Luther had
(teauen yeares before, disafteroufly blinded by
an obscure aloud of darksome Herefie, raised
in Germanie. For, in the kingdome of Mexico
alone, were numbred so many Christians, that
the Chronologer Amandus Ziritikeus affir-
med, that *Fere cum Ecclesia Latina comparari posset Ecclesia illa Indica.* One might then al-
moft compare the Indian Church with that of
the Latin. This holy Father was of the Prouince of S. Gabriel, where he knew by reuelation, that the Childrē of that Prouince should
profit much in the conuersion of the Indians;
the which prophecie is now totally accom-
plished in those our holy Martyrs: For whose
fake we write this Historie. For from out of

the Prouince of S. Gabriel was founded that of
S. Ioseph, from whence these our poore dis-
called Martyrs tooke their iourney towards the
Indies: where it seemes that by Almightie God,
the Catholicke Church, and the Christian
Kings were all Apostolically bent: and in this
exploite imitated that potent Monarch A-
lexander the Great, who stripping naked those
choise souldiers whom he had expressely selected for the conquest of the world, said, that
by how much they were poore and naked ex-
teriouly, by so much more would they be animated to fight couragiously to obtaine des-
poiles of their enemies, and lesse enuied of their
foes. This was the reason that the poore (in
transitory riches but in Charity abounding)
Order of S. *Francis* was honoured with the first
onset of this generous assault, to be vndertaken
against a new world, the Indies: Hauing therefore, to this purpose crossed the turbulent Seas
with the first armes of the King of Portugal
and Spaine, they did there most Apostolically
Euangelize the holy Gospell of *Iesus Christ*, as
well in nature of Preachers, Pastors, Bishops,
Archbishops, and Apostolicall Legats, as in qualitie of trustie Embassadours from Kings and
Emperours, yea, from the very Infidells themselues, and their whole kingdome, planting
therein the triumphant tree of the holy Crosse,
the which since hath so budded, and shot forth
its sacred branches (watered with the bloud
of their bodies and sweate of their browes)

that

that they haue there engrafted both Palmes
and Bayes, whereof to wreath illustrious
Laurels, and glorious garlands for triumphant
Martyrs: Which as they all first budded and
sprung from the precious bloud of our Sauiour
Iesus Christ, so the children of S. *Francis* from
the bloud of their Seraphicall Father, in such
manner conioyned to that of Iesus Christ, that
(although in Valētia it be farre vnequall) yet at
least it doth so helpe forward the effect, as that
it animates the Children thereof to the same
generous encounter like as the warlike Eli-
phant is as much encouraged at the sight of
the bloud of a simple and common souldier, as
of a great and valiant Captaine. Would you
euer beleiue that the bloud of S. *Francis* his
Stigmats hath some participation with that
of *Iesus-Christ*? Howbeit his bloud was shed
by the rage of his enemies, but this of S. *Francis* by the hand of Iesus - Christ himselfe. Yes
truely, our Lord opened his side (like to that
of Adam) to ingrafte a fertile generation of
holy Martyrs. A little before the deaths of
these holy Martyrs, an Image of S. *Francis* was
seene by them in the Citie of Meaco, miraculously all running with bloud, signifying their
cruell and blouddy deaths, which should water the Countrie of Iaponia, in such aboundant
máner, as that the people of all those Isles were
in the end both wholly and happily fortunate,
by the totall conuersion of all those who were
sōmoned, by thē, into the Court of the Church

of God. Thus farre out of the forefaid Author.

But of thofe acts in the Indians or of thofe
of thefe latter ages performed by thē for your
fuller content in all particulars, you may perufe
Charles Rapineus his hiftory of the Apoftoli-
call acts atchieued by the FF. Minors in Eaft
and Weft Indies compiled in 10. bookes alfo
the Hiftory of the 2 3, Protomartyrs of Iaponia of the Order of S. *Francis*, fee alfo the Hiftory of the conuerfion of the new Mexico a
moft fpatious countrey containing many Prouinces, and Territoryes founde out & couerted
by the Freer Minors of S. *Francis*: this Hiftory
is in diuers languages within thefe 3. yeares to wit
Spanish, French, and Latine, fee alfo Marianus his Francifcus Rediuiuus or S. *Francis* Re-
uiued: alfo D. Eftius his Hiftory of the Gor-
chom Martyrs, Thom. Buchier his Ecclefiafticall hiftory of the Freers Martyred in England,
Scotlād, & Irelād, alfo a booke intituled *Lucer-
na Fidei accenfa per Fratres Minores in Palatinatu
& alijs Prouincijs Germaniæ* wherin by the te-
ftimonies and letters of the Emperour, Duke
of Bauariæ, Lords. and Magiftrats of diuers ter-
ritories Cities, townes, and villages (before
thefe laft warres) is declared that the Freer
Minors conuerted thofe teritoryes, Cityes,
Townes and Villages and therfore reprehends
fome that would enter in to their harueft, to
reape glory where they neuer had fowne, for
this is particular to this Order that alwayes it
addicted it felfe rather to acte and doe, then

*Authors
that
haue re-
corded
the me-
morable
acts of
the FF.
in thofe
later ages*

to

to depredicate their owne actions in writing,
no wayes placing there glory in the mouths of
men yea hiding oftentimes that which is necessary, of which the Psalmist speakes w en
he sayd O Lord silence not my prayse for
that the mouth of the deceitfull is opened a
gainst me.

It is not my purpose to declare that after
S. *Francis* had vnderstood by the reuelations
made to S. *Clare* and B Siluester that his vocation was not only to contemplate but by exãple
& doctrine to benefit his neighbour he forth-
with went to preach & parting his 8. religious
(which then he only had)in forme of a crosse
he sent them ouer the 4.quarters of the world
where they fructified so much as that when by
the Saints desire they miraculously assembled
to the Chapter there were present 5000.
whēce you may gather how much the prãmē
tioned 8. proffited, and how many were extracted out of the diuels iawes, since that so many
were conuerted to this pœnitentiall and Apostolicall Order.

In the expedition of this Chapter S. *Francis* desirous in a more particular manner to renew the birth of all mankind, departed all the
Christian and Pagan Coūtries, of the world to
his brethren, whose merites, seruices, and labours for the exaltation of gods Church, how
many & how great they were I remit you to the
R. & renowned F. Fa. Luke Wadding: Annales,
where not only those, but also infinite other la-

Psal. 61
c.18.
Chron.
1. c 10.
S. Bon.
l. 4. in
V. S. Fr.

Chro. 1.
part.
Pisanus
lib. de
Conform
fruct. 19
& 24.

bours

bours and deserts of theirs you may finde re-
giftred. In the expedition of the aforesayd
Chapter the Saracens fell to S. *Francis*, wither
he repaired with his companions and coming
thither he made the Great Soldan of a Lyô & a
woolfe (who would haue giuen before to any
that should bring a Chriftians head a great recompence) a meeke lambe graunting licence to
him and his Companions to preach the Gofpell
in his Dominions, defiring the Saint to pray for
him, which he did for as S. Antonine of Florence reports he was baptized by his religious
after the Saints departure, of whô God hauing
ordained that he should not only be a light to
the Gentiles but alfo renew his life and the memory of his paffion in the hearts of the faithfull, he returned into Europe where in Italy
vpon Mounte Aluerne on the feaft of the Exaltation of the Croffe, it pleafed out B. Sauiour
to make him remarkable by the impreffion of
his facred woundes which with exceffiue paine
for 2 yeares till his death he bore vifibly in
his body, but omitting thofe *Magnalia Dei* as not
able noi worthy to depredicate them. It shall
fuffice me, to exhibite in a trafitory view fome
generall notions of this Order, felected out of
the Chronographicall Table which *Vitalis de
Alg-Zira* by the approbation of Malderus
Bishop of Antwerpe published 1616.

In this there are rekoned 27. Canonized
Saints which is much both for the time of the
Order, and alfo for the difficulty of Cannoni

zation

zation which not lóg before S. *Francis* his time was vsed with such streight and rigorous examination. but before the Bishops, and Prelats, of the places approbatió of theirs sáctity sufficed. Of beatified 606. & of Confessours renowned for Sanctity and Miracles 1650. but what doth he say 1650. since according to the allegation of Rappeneus. The Prince of the Canonists D Nauarre, and S. Vincent the ornament of the Dominicans, *affirme that there neede no miracles to canoniZe the professours of the Rule of the Freer Minors, who by the sole obseruance of their Rule may without feare (say they) be published for Saintes, in so much as a Pope did say if he did cannoniZe those which were saintes of this Order, it was behoofull he should register in the role of SS. all those which remained in the Obseruance of their profession, and that the See Apostolique would haue emploiment enough theriuonly, and that there would not be sufficient dayes in the yeare to giue euery one his due honour apart.* To wit so great is the perfection of this Euangelicall Rule dictated to S. *Francis* by *Christ Iesus* Master of perfection, as it not only placeth his Obseruers assuredly in heaue, but it also eleuates them to a most eminent degree of glory: as the testimony of our all-Immaculate Virgin our B. Lady to Robert Maidston, Bishop of Hereforde (related by Wadding) confirmes: for as you may reade in that Author when our Lady had shewne him in a vision all the mansions of glory correspondent to euery ones state, at last

Rapin. in the beging of his Chron.

Nota

r. Tom. Annal. Christ loueth the Freers particularly.

G   shee

shee shewed him the F. Minors immediatly vnder hir sonne telling him *that Christ loued them more then any other, for that they had perfectly imitated his life,* And with all exhorted him for the greater security of his saluation to make himselfe a member of that Order, which he did afterwards relinquishing his Bishopprike, as also did many other grand personages in that kingdome as namely Cloptome Lord cheife Iustice of England, the Lord Lile, the Lord Abot of Abington, the Abot of Osne. in a word, not only seculars but also religious namely Benedictines, Augustines, yea and Carthusians (as the Ecclesiasticall history of England witnesseth,) flowed vnto it: so great was the estimatiō of this Order there, and so perfect a conformitie it was iudged to haue with Christ and the Apostles life, the paterne and Rule of discerning the eminency in perfections as that F. Minors there were styled and called for many yeares by the name of the Order of the Apostles. Of Martyrs he numbers 9*to.* although indeed they are innumerable: Abot Ioachim with a Propheticall spirit foretold many things of S. Dominike and S. Francis, as also of their Orders: speaking of the FF. Minors and recounting a many Countries they should passe into at last sayeth that a great part of them should goe to heauen by Martyrdome and indeed it is a thing so proper and frequent to this Order as that when S. *Francis* (though he passed to the Saracens Country to that end,

howbeit

Harsfild. in vita Io. Pecham. Freers in England called the Order of the Apostles. Wadd. tom. 1. martirs apud Vaddingum tom. x.

howbeit God ordained for him a farre more
glorious Martyrdome to wit to beare the sacred and dolorous Wounds of *Iesus Christ*) whē
he heard the newes of some of his Brothers
missionized to Moroco to haue bene put to
death, he sayd he thanked God that now he
had ƒ true F. Minors, and it is a condition proposed publikly to those that will professe this
Rule , that it occasiō presēts it selfe, whither
they would be ready to vndergoe Martyrdome
or no? to which if they answere affirmatiuely
the Superior giues, him his professiō. Whēce it
is no wōder if at the breach with the Apostolicall
See made by King Henry the 8. that not one,
but all the obseruant Freer Minors in England
(*Omnes ad vnum* saith *Alanus Copus ana Surius*)
were persecuted, and as D. Sanders relates were
all put out of their Monasteries before the
least persecution was raised against any other
Orders : and at one time about 200· were in
London prisons when as by all humble suppli-
cations, efficacious and conuincent arguments
they could not peaceably maintaine the vniō of
England with the Church of Rome , and re
gaine the King whom they so honoured, and
whom the King before his reuolt (moued by
the example of his Father Henry the 7. who
for his singular deuotion to the Order builded
and erectect for them 6. Monasteries) as that he
elected them to be the spirituall directors and
Ghostly Fathers both to himselfe & his Queene
Margaret of the ʒ. Order of S. *Francis* from

Chron·
tom. **1.**

Surius
in Cōm.
de rebus
in orbe
gestis
Sanders
lib. de
scism.
Anglica
Stepha-
nus Ba-
ronis
Was
Henr:
the 8.
Ghostly
Father
an F.
Iohn
Forest
marty-
red and
so shi
no was
the
Queene

whom he would haue bene diuorced: which
designe, when by the prementioned meanes the
Freers could not hinder, complying with their
obligations towards God in so necessa y a
cause, publickly in their sermons impugned it,
as also those who for worldly ends adulato
riously smoothed vp the King in his pretece:
for which cause King Henry the 8. put so ma
ny of them to death, partly publickly, partly by
poisoning them and smothering them with
the lothsomefilth in the dungeons in as that
hauing considered well their candide and pure
good intentions towards him, and also the
grounded motiues on which they founded the
selues: ingeniously confessed at the houre of
his death that his proceedings towards the
Franciscans, more grieued him then all that he
had done against other Orders, as witnesseth
Thomas Bouchier (sometimes in great grace
with Queene Elizabeth) in his Ecclesiasticall
History of those Martyrs passions.

Of those whose worth and merites hath
aduanced to Ecclesiasticall prelacy: 6. Popes,
12. Patriarkes, 57. Cardinals, 128. Arch
bishops, 590. Bishops. Hieronimus Romanus
affirmes that there are not 4. bishoppriks in all
the dominions of Spaine which hath not had
a Freer for their Bishop. Yea as I am credi
bly informed by a man of quality, one Conuent
of Salamanca in Spaine within these 3. yeares
hath afforded 8. Freers which I say within these
3. yeares were all actually Bishops.

*Sanders
ls. de
Sym.
Angl.
The mul
ttude
of En-
glish
martyrs.
Henr. 8.
more
forresfor
his perse
cution
against
the Freer
then any
others
tho Bou-
chier.
The Ec-
clesiasti-
call Pre
lats the
Order
hath af-
forded
the
Church.*

Of Apostolicall Legats and kings Embaſ-
ſadours for to negotiate Eccleſiaſticall affaires
for the Churches conſeruation and exaltation, are numbred 270.

Of great perſonages which haue adorned
this Order or rather hath bene adorned by its
eminency: as wel to this purpoſe ſaith the moſt
illuſtrious Cardinall Treio in his Epiſtle
prefixed to *S. Francis* his works. Where hauing
vttered many rare and excellent things of *S.
Fracis.* & his 3. Order: in the end he ſayth: what
need many words? is not the gray or aſhco-
lour habit of *S. Francis* truly purple wherwith either regall or Cardinall Excellécy may
be adorned? that is truly purple which Chriſts
bloude hath ſigned and the beleiſe of his paſſô
hath dyed, & which inſteed of *Chriſt S. Francis*
with his owne bloud flowing from his ſacred
wound hath ſcarleſied and died red? is the
humility of Chriſt, ſeruitude? &c. of ſuch grand
perſons I ſay are counted 2. Emperours 4. Em-
preſſes, 20. Kings, amongſt whom was King
Iohn of Armenia who was Soueraigne maiſter
to 24. crowned Kings vnder him of whom the
Poet Sang

*Armenia wonders at their King of Royall ſeede
Caſting downes ſcepter and clad in S. Francis
weede.*

Of Queens 20. the ſonnes and daughters of
Kings 55. 1. Archiduke, 7. Princes, 20. Dukes,
34. Marquiſſes, of Counts 85. of Archidu-

G 3   cheſſe

Great perſons rather illuſtra-ted by this Order then that they ennoble is

chesses 1. of Princesses 7. of Duchesses 46.
Marquisses 26. Countesses, 32. Sonnes and
daughters of such Nobles 368. of Inquisitors
which conserues Religion and represseth the
licencious liberty of Hereticks broaching new
paradoxicall and damnable opinions are rekoned 84. without counting those which are Ordinarily from the yeare 1258. at Spoleto, Fulginia Reate, Florence, Veuice, Ragutio, Istriæ,
Bosnæ and Dalmatia. Of famous writers in di
uers sciences, which haue bene burning lamps
of wisdome extending their lustre ouer the
whole world, more then 880. amongst whom
where the three founders of Schoole Diuinity,
and that to the Singular glory of our Nation
all English men, namely Alexander Hales Ge-
neral of the Realists, and Master vnto S. *Bona-*
uenture and S. *Thomas* of Aquine, both branches
of his schoole, 2. Iohn Dunscot Author of the
Formalists 3. William Ocham Prince of the
Nominals schoole, Whose merits and commé-
dations are to be prized according to the vnspeakable benefit of diuinity brought to that
Methode and perfection by them which all
Prelats & Pastours yea the whole Church doe
abundantly experience.

The great compasse and extent of the Order
côpriseth 181. Prouinces. 31. Vicaries, schooles
in the Indies to teach not boyes only but also
men and boyes, and that not Grammer for
(which ther are Pedagogs enough euery where)
but Christian Doctrine, in which they Imitate

Christ

[marginal notes:]
Inquisi-
tors.

Famous
Doctors.

The
Foúders
of Schole
diuinity
English.

The
great-
nesse of
the Or-
der

Chriſt and his Apoſtles who are neuer reade to
haue taught boyes Grammer: The diſciple is
perfect if he imitate his Maſter and according
to our Maſter *Chriſt Ieſus* the diſciple is not a
boue the Maſter. Of Conuents their are numbred 9336. of Religious of this order (omitting
the Tertiaries of S. *Francis* which are innume
rable) the laſt Generall chapter at Rome Ann.
1625. euery Prouinciall giuing vp the number
of the Br. & Fat. which were in their Prou.)
there were nūbred 28379̃3. In ſo much that
in the time of Calixt° the 3 Pope of that name
1455. in the raigne of Fredericke the 4. The
Generall obliged himſelfe to giue thē 30000.
Ffeers if they would make holy warre againſt
the Infidels and Pagās maintaining the Quires
with as many more &c. *Ex huius Ordinis Soda-
litio* Saith Roderiquez *viri per celebres exortiſunt,
qui & ſanctitate, & vitæ integritate cum doctrina
excellentia coruſcarunt: ita vt nulla vel frequentior,
vel amplior monaſtica profeſſio ipſis Minoribus in
Ecclesia habeatur,* Seldome ſaith M. *Antonius
Coccius Sabellius* and I know not whether euer
I ſpoke more true, no Order or inſtitute of humaine pietie, euer had ſo great a propagation as
this one family which hath filled & Poſſeſſed the
whole world: yea ſaith that great Glory of the
Dominicans Granada *Tantum abſuit vt a Beato
Franciſco inſtitutus ordo inopia cogente defecerit*
(Note the ſequel) *vt ob hoc ipſum ſupra omnes a-
lios Ordines auctus ac dilatatus fuerit, &c. Hinc
factum eſt vt vnicus Beatiſſimi Patris Frāciſci Or-*

*Roderi-
quez.t.1
Vbi ſup.*

*No Or-
der ſo
much
ampli-
fied as
F. Min.
Enn. 9.
li. which
Con. 2.
de S. Fr.
Accor-
ding te
Grana-
do S. Fr
Order*

do

hath more houses then all the other Orders togeather. S. Francis seemes to haue Iacob benediction.

do plura fortaſſe inter ſe cænobia, quam reliquⁱ omnes omnium aliorum Ordinum contineat. We may therfore pioully beleeue that God almighty whoſe conuersation is with thoſe that are ſimple, gaue the like benedictiō to the Patriarke S. Francis for his doues innocency as he gaue vnto the Patriarke Iacob for his gratefull ſimplicity (*Gen. 24.*) Iacob was a ſimple man and dwelt in the tabernacles to whom (*Gen. 18.*) God conferred this bleſſing ſaying *thou ſhalt be dilated and ſpread from Eaſt to weſt, from North to South and all the Tribes of the Earth ſhall be bleſſed in thy ſeede, and I will alwayes be with you wherſoeuer you ſhall walke.* And indeed God could not but be with him that hath peopled heauen with Saints, not only by the multitude of the Profeſſours of his Order, but alſo of others in all Parts of the world, by the induſtrious labour of him & his childrē plucked forth out of the iawes of the infernall deuouring Dragō and conſecrated and wholy dedicated to God, ſo that in his ſeed all tribes vpō the face of the Earth hath bene bleſſed and made happy: and as it may be ſayi of S. *Francis* (whom ſome termes the Second precurſor of Chriſts 2. comingto witthe day of Iudgment) *there was a man ſent from God whoſe name was Iohn* (ſo S. *Francis* his name in Baptiſme was Iohn, though afterwards changed not without miſterie) by whō I meane by himſelfe and his Order all Nations ſhould beleeue & be taught, ſo likewiſe with out offéce may be ſayd of the Order

(of him

(of him who had as many conformityes with Christ, as was possible for a creature with his Creator) that which is sayd of Christs Church for the manifold grace therin *Quosdam dedit Apostoles quosdam Prophetas*, &c. to wit, there *Stood a Queene at his right hand in a vestiment of gold, compassed with variety,* so that may be applied not vnfitly to this Order that shee is *Christ Iesus* the King of Kings his poore Darre. and Espouse, compassed With the variety of Martyrs, Doctors, Confessors, and Apostolicall men &c. as also by the multiplicity of families, to wit Conuentuales, Obseruantines, and Capucines, *inuested with gold,* that is with ardent Charity, for the abondance of which towards God & their neighbour so effectually demonstrated, this Order by the Church is inuested with the title of *Seraphicall:* and though all Orders haue their proper Ornaments and multiplication according to that (24. *of Num.*) *Pulchra sunt omnia tabernacula Iacob qua fixit Deus quasi Cedros prope aquas,* for God is the founder of all religious Orders *ipse fundauit & multiplicauit eos, &c.* Yet by the way of excellency saith Roderiquez, the Church singeth of no other Order, that which it singeth of S. *Frācis* to wit *Deus qui Ecclesiam tuam Beati Francisci meritis fœtu noua prolis amplificas &c.* For not onely in the beginning it spread it selfe, & produced worthy persons and pillars of the Church, but as *Hieronymus Platus* the Iesuite saith *not only that Age wherin this Order sprung*

Psalm. 44.

F. Minors styledby the Church the Seraphicall Order. All Ordershath their prope Excellencys. Eze 37. Platus. l.2.c.30.

H vp₂

vp, was wonderfully enlightned and holpen by it, but it hath euer strengthned and vpheld the Church of God these 376. yeares which it hath continued since the first beginning, & indeed if wee consider impartially what this Order hath done in the Indies, in the Conuersion of Gentiles, in the conseruation of the holy Land & the sepulcher of our B. Sauiour, wherof they only are Guardians and keepers, with many labours and the spilling of much bloud in the Turks Countryes, as also the great opposition they haue made against the Churchs enemies, not only by writings but also with the losse of their liues, in France, the low Countryes, Germany, England, Scotland and Ireland &c. you will affirme with Grauinus the Dominican a Doctor in Diuinitie that S. Francis his Order doth as much now flourish in her old age as shee did in her youth and first feruour. & hereby the way, I can not but greatly admire the wisdome of Gods prouidence that as Martin, Luther by preaching all carnall liberty and impugning all mortifications of the body and humiliations of our selues, peruerted many weake soules: so did he raise vp an other Martin, to wit, de Valétia of the family of the F. Minors Recollects of S. Fraci, who about the same time by diuine prouidence superadded vnto the Rule many streight and austere Cóstitutiós of life, by which they conserued, conuerted and regained more soules to God, then the Heretikes by their licentious Gospel liberty (as

they

the Freer keeps the holy lãd and sepulcher of Christ.

they tearme it)peruerted and withdrew. So
this Order alwayes enlargeth ſtregneth &ſup
porteth Gods Church by the Exaple of S. *Fran-*
cis their Generall, of whom the Ornament of
Cardinales Baronius, Depoſeth inthis māner
(God compaſſionating the miſeries of this la-
mentable world, and fully decreeing to repaire
and vphold his Church declining worſe and
worſe, and euen falling by the depraued diſcipline of māners, Framed in the fornace of the
holy Ghoſt, this Apoſtolicall mā Frācis, as a new
ſtarre ro diſſipate the darke cloudes of ſinne
and error.) Whence Hen: ab Vrimar an Augu-
ſtine Saith that S. *Francis* had three beames by
which he illumina ted the whole world &c. &
that of him is verified that which is written in
Ecc les 43. *Tripliciter ſol exurens montes radios*
igneos exuflans & refulgens. For ſaith he, by the
beame of Doctrine, he diſpelled ignorance, by
the beame of Example he baniſhed negligence
from the Tepide and ſhouggiſh: and by the
beame of Miracles, he vanquiſhed obſtinacy
and obduracy. Wherfore ſince this Order is ſo
fertile a ſoile & hath ſuch an excellēt ſeedmā as
was S. *Francis* with what temerity can any
one either directly or indirectly villiſye this
ſtate, or detract from the profeſſors thereof
eſpecialy ſince (as *Nicholas* III. Pope pro-
nounceth.) *They are the profeſſors of that holy*
Rule which is founded in the Euangelicall worde,
authenticated by the Example of Chriſts life, and ra-
tified by the ſpeeches and actes of the Apoſtles, foun-

Sorm. 3.
de S.
Francis.

6. decre.
de verb.
ſig. exit.
qui. &c.
Pope
Nicholas
his Com-
menda-
tion of
the Rule
and Or-
der.

H 2   *dations*

dations *of the militant Church. That it is with God* (howsoeuer Carnall libertines esteeme therof) *a pure and Imaculat Religion, which descending from the Father of light, deliuered verbaly and exemplary to the Apostles by the Sonne, and finally by the holy Ghost inspired and reuealed to S. Francis and his followers: hath the testimoniall of the whole Trinity, and that it is that which by the attestatiō of S. Paul No man hereafter ought to molest* (to with malice or persecutiō) *seeing Christ by the stigmats of his passion hath confirmed it, in making its Institutor remarkable by the signets his passion,* The impressiō of which stigmats called by *Bellarmine segnum omnium maximum ac singulare & quasi prodigium omnium prodigiorum,* The Church highly honours with an anniuersary solemnity. By this (Pious Reader) you may easily collect how great a Fauorite of God S. *Clares* Instructor was, pointed vndoubtedly out by S Iohn in his Apocalips (as most euidently demonstrats Vicounte Montague of pious memory in his Epistle prefixed to his Translation of *saint Francis his life*) whē he said I *saw an other* Angel (to wit S. *Francis* an Angelicall man for the eminency of his vertues) *ascending from the rising of the sonne* (to wit like an other morning sonne continually waxing more resplendent, illuminating by himselfe and his followers the whole vniuerse) *hauing the signe or image of the liuing God* (to wit, for so great a conformity as was compatible with the limitatiō of a Creature to his Redeemer Iesus Christ (as wel

demonstrates

demóstrates Bart. Pifan, in a whole booke of that
argumé,) wee may alfo fee how due to S. *Fräcis*
as was fayd in the begi íg, is the title of *Repairer
of Gods Church.* All which *Gregor. 9.* to æternalize
and perpetuate the memory of tne S. hath con-
firméd by a Funerall monumét on S. *Francis* his
fepulcher, which I wil here fubfcribe as a finall
claufe: if firft I fatiffie the interrogatory which
fome make, to wit, how could **S.** *Francis* and
his Order be fuch great pillars of Gods Church,
when they feeme to be fimple and poore, ha-
uíg neither riches, wealth, nor power? Grauin⁹
the Dominican *in 2. parte* of his *Vox Turturis
c. 14.* anfwereth well this queftió whé he faith,
that among other Miracles God hath wrought:
that is moft eminent, that hefubdued the world
and the wifdome therof by a few fimple men,
fo by the *Freer Minors,* he confoundes the va-
nity and pompe of the world *Confider* (faith he
out of S. *Paul*) *not many powerfull, or noble
according to the flesh, but God chofe the Weake of the
world to confound the ftrong: and the ignoble
and contemptible, and the things which are not,
to deftroy the things which are:* for which S. *Paule*
giues this reafon *that all flesh may not Glory,* at-
tributing to humain forces which is to be guë
to God. And indeed God is not chaçged in the
courfe by which he now conuerted the New
World America then anciently he did the
Olde, as well oferueth *Platus à Candido* Author of the Iefuits l. 2. c. 30. Who in the fame
worke, fayes that the Francifcás not only pro-

moted the finding out of it, but were the first
Conuerters of it, whom also in the same
chapter he affirmes, to haue bene the first of
the East Indies also. To speake much in a few
words, saies Gonsaga Bishop of Mantua *what
soeuer labours in the East Indies for* 40. *continuall
yeares either in Curing the infirme, or in conuerting
the Infidels, or in instructing the Cathecumists, or
cultiuating the reconciled, either in the admi-
nistration of the Sacraments or in the exercise of
other Charitable works that all lay vpon the
shouldiers of the Franciscans (Hist. Seraph. p. 4.)* so
that the iyce was broken by them *dimidium
facti qui bene cæpit, habet.* Which also is farther
confirmed out of Turseline the Iesuite *l. 2. vita
S. Xauer. Nulli quippe in tota India tunc erant
religiosi, præter eos quos dixi Franciscanos qui Christiana res nauabant operam.* And by the way to
omit how these Iesuites are to be accorded, for
Platus lets into the East Indies the Dominicans, and Augustines before the Iesuites, which
Turseline denies, saying that there were none in
all the Indies but Franciscās before S. *Xauerias*
his Arriuall, to omit this I say you must note
by the way that when Iesuites writes vnder S.
Xauier his picture as any other where *Apo-
stolus Indiarum &c.* or *Effigies B. Xauerij qui
primus è Societate fidem in India inuexit.* You
must know they doe not vnderstand, that he
was the first Conuerter of them, or that he was
first absolutely of all Orders that carried the
light of the Gospel into those partes, no but

that

Turse-
line in S
Xauer.
life l. 2.

'hat among many of the Society, that haue laboured there, he was the first Ieiuite, and therfore with relation to themselues he may be
sayd the first, which is spoken least any should
thinke that they (who direct all *ad Maiorem
Dei Gloriam*) may not be thought to arrogate
falsly, or æquiuocally that which *in Domino*
others may glorie for, seeing therfore *non est fa-
cienda vis* according to S. Austine *in verbis, vbi
constat de intentione*; and it is manifest according
to the testimonies of Platus and Turseline
both of the Society of the most holy name of
Ie*sus*: that the Franciscans were Gods first instruments in the conuersion of the Indians, none
ought to taske them of any iniury, they neither
intended or haue done, in such or the like
writings. God therfore vnchangeable in the
course for the couerting the new & old world
as he chose the Apostles poore and simple
men, for the first conuersion of the old world,
so for the first subduing the new world to the
yoke of Christ he elected the F. Minors men
of an innocent simplicity and destitute of all
humane power, *Confiteor tibi Pater Domine cœ-
li & terra, quia abscondisti hæc à sapientibus &
prudentibus* (opinione propria) *& reuelasti ea par-
uulis* (rebus temporalibus vel sensu malitiæ:) The
second reason why the Freers state is so proper to fructifie, is drawne out of S. Chrisostome and it reflecteth vpon the men that are
to be holpen who are more moued by exāple
of life then words alone. And here we speake

not of what may be, but what is more forcible
to perſwade and winne peoples hearts. For
who can make any doubt, but that people
will eaſier beleeue that a man ſets all humane
things at naught, if they ſee him indeed contemne them, then if outwardly they ſee no
ſuch thing by him, though inwardly in his
minde he be ſo diſpoſed, which men can not
know becauſe they can not diue into the ſe-
crets of our hearts? but let vs heare what the
Golden ſpoken Father S. Chriſoſtome ſpeakes
to this purpoſe *Hom. 46. in Matth.* If twelue
men, *ſaith he*, were able to conuert the whole
world, think with yourſelues, how great our
wicked-eſis, who cannot reforme our owne
ſubiects, being ſo manie of vs, that we might
ſuffiſe for ten or eleuen thouſand worlds. You
wil ſay, the Apoſtles wrought miracles. But it
was not their miracles, which made them ſo
much admired. For many ſinners did caſt out
Diuels, and wrought no ſuch effects, but were
puniſhed, What was it then which made them
ſo great? the contempt of money, the deſpiſing
of honour, the abſtaining from all buſineſſes of
this life; if they had not had theſe things,
though they had raiſed the dead, they would
not only not haue holpen any bodie, but bene
eſteemed ſeducers. Thus farre S. Iohn Chry
ſoſtome moſt properly to the commendation
of the F. Minors, who as they are moſt eminent
in the vow of Obedience as promiſing particularly to Obey the Pope, and their ſuperiorus

in

Note
wel.

in al things which are not sinnefull & against
their Rule; so doe they surpasse in pouerty, not
only relinquishing dominion and propriety in
particular as all other Orders doe, but making
a perfect renunciation in common also, con
tenting themselues with the bare vse of things
with out any propriety. And this to the end
that being wholy abstracted from terrene af
faires they the more strictly be vnited with
God and haue their conuersation in heauen, as
also for the loue of their neighbour, abandoning all dominion that they may haue no ian
glings or law suites with them, remouing all oc
casions which may effect any breach of
charity, with groūde being laid in themselues.
Tell me I pray can any man better exhorte an
other to the loue of God, then they that haue
giuen so euident testimony therof by relin.
quishing all for his sake? can any one better
incite one to the obeissance of the supreme
Pastor and other Prelats, then a F. Minor
who without President before them hath particularly obliged himselfe thereūto by a fourth
vow ? Can any more forceably persuade one
to imitate the pouerty of Christ (who saith
though, the birds haue their nests and foxes
their dennes yet the sonne of man hath not
wherwith all to shelter himselfe) then a F.
Minor who appropriates neither houses or any
thing at all, much lesse seekes after wealth and
riches , who is this? tell me who is this? and
wee will extolle him to the heauens for he

Bellar.

I hath

hath done wonders in his life. And this admirable contempt of riches seemed so strange to the Indians, as it was a singular motiue of

*In the F.
Minors.*

their conuersion as hath bene said in the aforegoing chapter. Who is he that can better incite one to the austerites and mortifications of the body, that according to S. Paul the life of Christ may be manifested in vs: then the F. Minors that are cladde in sakloth or poore contemptible habits, naked in there feet, hard in their lodging, in their diet auster, often fasting and praying night and day? Who can better propose vnto their Auditorie, the Humility of *Christ Iesus* then F. Minors, which in an eminent degree voluntarly misprize, and humble themselues, whence Innocent the 4. writing

W *add.
to. 1.ad
ann.*
124!.

W *add.*

to the Bulgarian king telles him that before all other he hath made choyse of F. Minors for that he iudged, they would be more beneficiall to him, in regard they were followers and imitators of Chrifts humility, In a word who can more effectually preach any euangelicall Precept or Counsel either for the purchase of virtue or extirpation of vice then whose profession and life is to obserue the Gospel? but such are the F. Minors *Regula & vita Minorū Fratrū hæc est scil. Domini nostri Iesu Christi Euangelium obseruare, ex cap.* 1. *Regula & vltimo* seeing therfore according to their parterne and master *Christ Iesus*, who as wholy writte recordes, begane to doe, and teach: they first practise in themselfes and then preach, que

stionlesse they wil be great in the kingdome of
heauen *Qui facit & docet hic Magnus vocatitur in
Regno cælorum* for the haruest of many soules
they shall reape by that manner of preaching,
& he that will be greatest amōgst Christ Disci-
ples let him be Minor minor I say in all temporall substance and estimation of himselfe, so
that they prefix no terme or limite of such an
huble deicēt but that they be always Minor: to
wit, in theirowne estimatiō is he at litle as that
calles himselfe *Vermis & non homo & abiectio
plebis* a Worme and no man and the contempt
of the people? Minor lesser yet is he as litle as
he that for Gods sake renounceth all propriety
in particular, though not in Common. Minor
and so *in infinitum* with out limite in an humble
descent *qui enim se humiliat exaltabitur* he that
sominorizes himselfe shal highly be preferred:
this is the path their example and Master
Chrisl Iesus trode of whom saint Paul *quis est
qui ascendit nisi & qui descendit* who is he that as-
cends, to wit aboue all the heauens to glory
but he that descēded is minorised and made in-
ferior as it were to the Angels, which being
so *Dominicus Grauina* (Patrone of Religious and
paragon Defender of the faith of this age) in
his booke called V*ox turturis* worthyly saith
that the F. Minors profession, is *altissima, cælos
transit, par Angelis est, Angelicæ similis puritati*
and then in 392. page hauen recounted as a
thing worthy of admiration that the Turkes in
Palestine doth nourish aud maintaine diuers

Splendor
of the
Domini
cans p. 2
c. 14.

Conuents of this Order, to wit in Mounte
Sion, Ierusalem at the holy sepulcher, in
Bethlē, in the Valley of Iosaphat at Nazareth,
Mounte Oliuet, Bethania and at Iordaine, in
fine he attributes this singular prerogatiue vnto them for the perfect imitation and conformity they haue with Christs life let vs heare
him speake himselfe, *fiftly and congruently*
(saith he) *for the holy lande, our Lord hath elected
the Seraphicall Freers, seing that the holy land is the
house of God and Porte of heauen, therfore it is
beh fullst should haue such Ministers or seruants
Which in name and deed doe imitate the Cælestiall
ardent Seraphins, the custody of he cribbe where
Christ was poorely borne is due and aggreable to
those who professe pouerty in the highest degree.
The possession of the sepulcher With other places
where the wonders of Christ works are recorded Was
to be deputed to the Order of him in whose flesh
Were imprinted the Stigmats of Christ crucified, in
Mounte Oliuet and the Valley of Iosaphat, houses
Were to be assigned to them where he shall haue in a
readines the poore to iudge the twelue Tribs of Israel,
seing also We reade that the poore shall iudge.* Thus
he & least peraduēture you may thinke he doe
éxcede where he makes them pattakers of the
iudicatory power for their present voluntary
pouerty: haue though ! good to confirme
the same prerogatiue by the authority of many
Fathers *Saint Gregorie Nazianzen* in his O
ration against Iulian the Apostat, among other
praises of a Monastical life, reckoneth also,

that|

Iob. 36.

that they are to sit vpon Thrones to iudge. S.
Hierome in a certaine Epistle of his sayth: It is
proper to the Apostles and Christians to offer
them selues to God, and casting the mites of
their pouertie with the widdow into the
Treasurie of the Church, to deliuer all the
substance which they had to our Lord; and so
deserue to heare: *You shall sit vpon thrones iud-*
ging the twelue Tribes of Israel. S. *Augustin* (an
approued and sure Authour) sayth the same:
(They that haue not followed (sayth he) that
great and perfect Counsel of Perfection, o
Selling all, and yet keeping themselues free
from damnable crimes, haue fed our Saviour
in those that are hungrie, shal not sit on-high
to iudge with Christ, Neither must we thinke
that heauenlie Bench and Court shal haue but
twelue Iudges to sit, but by the number of
twelue, the whole generalitie is expressed) for
whosoeuer sait S. Gr. spurred on with the loue
of God, shal leaue his possessios, shal doubtles
obtaine a high seate of Iudicature, coming as a
Iudge together with the Iudge, because in
consideration of that Iudgement he punished
himselfe here by volutarie Pouertie. Venerable
Bede (an approued & learned Author) is not to
be omitted. He discoursing of this promise of
our Saviour in S. *Matthew*, of which he had
o ten spoken, sayth in this manner: A iust reward, that they, who for Christ contemned
here the glorie of humane preferment, should
there be glorifyed by Christ, sit as Iuges in spe-

eial commiſſion with him. And let no man
thinke, that only the twelue Apoſtle shal then
be Iudges, becauſe, after the fal of Iudas. S.
Matthias was choſen in his roome: as there be
not only twelue Tribes to be iudged: for els
the Tribe of *Leui*, which is the thirteenth,
should ſcape vniudged; and S. *Paul*, who is
the thirteenth Apoſtle, should be depriued of
his place of Iudicature; whereas he ſayth: *Doe
you not knꝛ w that we shal iudge the angeli?* For
we muſt know that al they, that according to
the example of the Apoſtles, haue left al they
had, and followed Chriſt, shal come with him
as Iudges, as al man-kind is to be iudged. For
becauſe by the number of Twelue in holie
Scripture the generalitie is often ſignifyed,
therefore by the twelue Seates of the Apoſtles
the generalitie of all them that shal iudge and
by the twelue Tribes of Iſrael the generalitie
of them that shalbe iudged, is expreſſed vnto
vs.) O fauour of familiaritie! O heigh of honour! O priuiledge of confidence! O prerogatiue of perfect ſecuritie! S. (*Bernar. ſer. qui babi-
tas*) Happie is the voluntarie Pouertie, my
Lord Ieſu, of thoſe that haue forſaken al, and
followed thee Doubtles a moſt bleſſed Pouer
tie, which makes men ſo ſecure, yea ſo glo
rious in that ſo hideous a diſſolution of the ele
ments, ſo feareful a trial of deſerts, ſo doubtful
an expectation of iudgemēt.) Which priuiledge
as you may read in the **Cronikles** of the **Freer**
Minors, by God was graunted to S. *Francis* and

his

tus Order.

Pardon me (Gentle reader) if ſhaue curti-
lized the Maieſty of this Order and exhibited
it in ſo tranſitory a view, for it was neuer my
intent to vndertake in a few pages to declare
that which many Authors in diuers volumes
though departing there labours (ſome for the
hiſtory of the ſaints others for famous acts
others for the deſcriptiõs of Prouinces others
for famous Writers &c.) yet were neuer able
to at cheiue or compaſſe it. To ſome peraduenture I may ſeeme to tedious, but let them
know I was enforced to it partly by the vniuſt
calumniations of ſome who thinkes that this
and other Orders are *inutilia terræ pondera &c.*
(for other Orders they I doubt not but when
oecaſion ſerue wil both celebrate and defende
themſelues hauing men of rare talents) for my
part incited by the example of the Pſalmiſte
in ſuch a caſe who ſaies *Deus laudem meam ne
tacueris: quia os peccatoris & os doloſi ſuper me
apertum eſt*, though I claime not the prerogatiue of the beſt abilities yet I haue endeauo-
red to put the brightſome light of the F. Minors from vnder the buſhel of the malignant
tongues and pennes who labours to obſcure
them, and I haue deſired to place it one the
candleſtick that all may in a manner ſee their
good works, and glorifie the Father in heauen
all which I haue performed out of approued
good authors without diſparaging any other
Order who haue euery one their proper ex-

cellency, but only shewing without comparison that they haue such attributes as may
ranke them amongst those Orders which are
esteemed most perfect and beneficiall, without
denying euery one in his kinde to be most perfect: partly also and principally that it may appeare that *S. Clare* (whose history wee now publish to the view of the world) receiued hir
Rule from so highly dignified a Patriarke who
deseruedly is styled the Repairer of Gods
Church as is pemomstrated before and now is
farther confirmed by the funerall monument
Gregory the 9. put. vpon the S. Shrine which
I haue put for a final onclusion of this chapter

Epitaphium sepulchri B.P. Francisci.

V. S. C. A.
Francisci Romani
Celsa humilitate conspicui
Christiani orbis fulciamenti
Ecclesiæ reparatoris
Corpori nec viuenti nec Mortuo
Christi Crucifixi plagarum
Clauorumq. insignibus admirando
Papa Nouæ feturæ collacrymans
Lætificans & exultans
Iussu, manu, munificentia posuit
Anno Domini M. CC. XXVIII.
XVI. Kalendas Augusti.
Ante Obitum Mortuus, post obitum viuus.

Quatuor litteræ capitales ita explicantur viri Sera-
phici, Catholici, Apostolici Romani vero dicitur Frã-
ciscus, summam erga Romanam Ecclesiam subie-
ctionem, constantemque erga Romanã fidem effectu.

Wadd.
swappes.
ad opus.
S. Fran.
S. Frãcis
pellar of
the Chri
stian
worlde &
Repaircr
of the
Church.

The institution of the Order of Sainte Clare.

CHAP. III.

OVR great God who doth tryumph, ouer whatsoeuer doth oppose his, power, and is author of Trophies and victories in heauen, in earth, and in hell: hath in all times in his Conquests made vse of weake Souldiers, and hath pleased to make choise of weake things, to confound the mighty of this world; the diuine Apostle, Doctor of the *Gentiles* and disciple of heauen astonished at so great a miracle, cryed out. The wisdome of this world is Folly before God, he hath chosen the foolish to confound the wise, as if he would say, the omnipotent (whose iudgements are inscrutable) hath chosen worldly ignoráce, & folly to cófound the wise and hath prepared to battle with the weakest forces, to surmoút and ouercome the strong & mighty: this was manifest in the holy Apostles, since I*esus Christ* our Redeemer for to surmount the furious and rauening wolues sent meeke and humble sheepe, which to humaine iudgment is most preposterous to send sheep in to the middest of wolues *Ecce ego mitto vos, si cut oues in medio luporum*, but this is the counsell of our great Captaine, and cheife generall that the conquest and victorie may be at-

I. Cor. 3

Matth. 10.

K   tributed

tributed to him, it is I that send you feare not
and it is my pleasure that your weaknes should
be the instrument of my glorie: truly this is the
strongest and most prodigious miracle, for
poore fisher men, ignorant, vnlearned, not
grounded in science and worldly wisdome,
preaching in simplicity without loftie subti-
litie or artificial Rethorick, to conuert the
wisest and subtilest Philosophers, and to bring
vnder the yoke of Christ the most Barbarian
and cruell nations, subiugating vnder the diuine
law the greatest Tirants and Potentats of the
earth: maintaining Gods cause with most forcible arguments, manfully denouncing and
proclaiming the truth to the Princes of the
earth, who captiuated by their Preaching ab
iured their false superstition wherin so many
yeares they had bene bredde, embracing the
new and vnknowne doctrine of these Aposto
licall Preachers the Diuell being compelled to
yeeld the field to these inuincible Champions,
no longer able to subsist in the presence of so
great a light, tooke his flight in to rhe caues
of horror and darknes.

The same Allmighty power and wisdome
of God is manifestly declared and most liuely
set forth in S. *Francis*, who was humble, des
pised of the world, without learning acquired
humaine, or diuine, his humility was so great
as he reputed himselfe the greatest sinner in the
world, trembling before the face of God, pas
sing whole nights in the repetition and pon-

deration

deration of the enfuing words; *Lord what art thou*, *and What am I*, thus annihilating himfelfe in comparifon of God there was not any thing that appeared fo vile and contemptible in his fight as himfelfe; for which cause God chofe him to vphold the frame of the militant Church which was shaken and ready to fall; fo as he repaired many breaches, caufed by the batterie and artillerie of the enemies (wherby many foules paffed to the feruice of *Satan*) repairing and fortifying them with the bull-works and trenches of Sanctitie, Humility, Obedience, Chaftity, Pouerty, and Contempt of the world.

But more fingularly hath our Lord made manifeft the greatnes of his power when this generous Captaine of the Chriftian warfare, not onely leuied souldiers of his owne company, but founding euery where the Allarum and trumpet, for to enrolle vnder the feruice of *Iefu Chrift* the weake Feminine fex, (by nature timerous, and fearfull,) who now with a manly, and generous courage, doe proclaime moft bloudie and implacable warre againft the powers of darknes, and the infernall Dragons, and all his complices; affranchifing them felues from his feruitude, infulting ouer him, by a glorious victorie, trapling him vnder foot defpicing all riches and voluptuous pleafures, to embrace profound humility, ftrict Pouerty, aufteritie of life, the abnegation of the will, and a life wholy Euangelicall.

76 The admmirable life

The institution of the Order of S. Cl.

Luc. Wadd. app.ar. 5. num. 12. Idem an 1253. §. 5

The words of sainte Clare in her testament

For the glorious Paranymph S. *Francis* the yeare 1212. by commandement of the Crucifix at S. *Damians* instituted an Order for woemen in all points like to the Freer Minors, the same in substance, words, and sentences, except some few points incompatible with their sex, the which six yeares before, replenished with a propheticall spirit he fortold when with feruor and diligence, he laboured in the reparation of S. *Damians* Church, *Assist for the loue of God in this building* (sayd the Saint to all passengers and beholders) *For this Church shalbe a Monasterie of poore Dames by whose life and renowne the heauenly Father shalbe glorifyed ouer all the world.* Behold the words of S. *Clare* in her testament, *With great ioy and illumination of the holy Ghost he Prophecyed of vs,* (to wit S. *Francis*) *that Which our Lord. Hath since fulfilled, for standing on the Walls of the sayd Church he called With a loud voice in the french tongue on some poore folks therby dwelling saying come help me in this Church of S. Damian: for there shall come woemon by Whose life and holy conuersation our heauenly father shall be honoured in his Whole Church.* Wherin Wee may marke the great bounty of God towards vs Who out of his aboundant mercy and charity did vouchsafe to Prophesie these things. By his seruant of our vocation and election and not only of vs did our holy Father foretell these things but also of those Who hereafter shall be partakers of the vocation Which our Lord hath called vs vnto.

Now the first of this generous enter-

prise

prife, was *Clare* an honorable Damofell of the
the Cytie of A*ſſiſſium* noble by race and extraction, but more illuſtrious and renowned for
her virtues, and heroyicall acts: the eldeſt
daughter of S. *Francis*, Mother of the Religious called Poore Clares or Dames of *Saint
Damian*, the bright mirrour of purity, and fanctity, the magazin, or ſtorehouſe of all virtue,
and perfection, ſeruing for an example to po-
ſterity, beating the way for many noble ſoules,
which by heauens decree, were to be enroled
vnder her lawes and diſcipline, conſecrating
their virginity to the heauenly ſpouſe. The
Rule which the Seraphicall father S. *Francis*
gaue vnto her was approoued by the ſoue-
raine Riſhops Innocent the third and Alexander the fourth.

The inſtitution of the third Order
Of Saint Francis called the
Order of pennance.

CHAP. IV.

THE glorious and Seraphicall Father
S. *Francis*, hauing inſtituted his fiſt Order of the Freer Minors, and ſoone after
the ſecond called the Order of S. *Clare*, was
much perplexed in mind wherefore often im-
parting this buſines with his moſt familiar

Brethren:

Brethren: he fayd vnto them, my deerest Brethren, I befeech you to giue me your aduife, which Were most conuenient to Gods honour, of these twe exercices, whether I should wholy apply my selfe to prayer, and contemplation, or by preaching to teach the ignorant the Way of saluation, in prayer wee speake to God, Wee heare him speaking to vs, and leading an Angelicall life, Wee conuers more in heauen with the Angells, then with men vpon earth, where on the contrary in preaching wee must conuerse with worldlings, liuing amongst them to conuert them and denounce the truth vnto them, hearing from them, many vaine and vnprofitable things neuertheles I behold how our Lord and Redeemer Christ Iesus who is the souueraine goodnes the Rule and modelle of diuine wisdome) hath taught and denounced the diuine doctrine, wherby he hath saued Soules Redeemed by his prettous bloud; for these confiderations I require your aduife and counsell, because our Lord hath neuer vouchsafed to reueale the same vntome, notwithstanding I haue dayly fought it of him with much instancie; the Religious replyed they were not capable to counsell him in this important affaire; the humble Francis with an inflamed Zeale of the diuine seruice willed Brother Mace to be called and sayd vnto him. Goe in companie of Brother Philip to our Sister Clare and bidd her from me, to present her prayers vnto God with all her Sisters beseeceing him to intimate vnto me his Diuine pleasure herein, and from thence goe vnto the mount Sabasio to seeke out Brother Syluester (whom the

holy

By prayer Wee speake to God.

S. Francis demands the assistance of the S. Cl. prayers

holy Ghost hath made worthy of the diuine communication, tell him, the same from me:

Brother Mace hauing executed his commissió, at his returne S. *Francis* receiued him with great charity washing his feet and preparing him to eat, then he ledde him to a mountaine, falling on his knees: his head vncouered and his armes extended in forme of a Crosse, expecting the precept of his God and Creator, sayd vnto Brother Mace *what is the will and pleasure of my Lord Iesus Christ.* Brother Mace replyed, brother *Siluester* falling to prayer receiued a reuelation from heauen. *that God had not called you to this vocation for your priuate profit but that by your predications many soules plunged in sinne might be conuerted vnto pennance,* And the same was reuealed vnto Sister *Clare* and this is the absolute wil of God: S. *Francis* but hearing these words of the will of God and vtility of his neighbour pronounced, answered *let vs goe in the name of God, Brother Mace, let vs goe,* and transported with feruour of spirit he presently began his way hauing taken Brother *Angelo* for a third, being now become the herauld of heauen, the terror of the earth, the trumpet of the Ghospell, the Patrone of penance, and consolation to the iust, ascourge to sinners, and a professed enemie to vice, proclaiming open warre against the flesh, the world, the diuel, and hell. He knew not whether he went but letting himselfe to be guided by the spirit of God, he arriued at a towne called *Cornerio*

a mile

S. Francis is called by God to conuert sinners.

a mile diftant from A*ſſiſium* planting the ftand
ard of pennance, there he preached to the
poeple with great feruor, & edification, from
all fides men and woemen, poore and rich,

Luc.
W *add.*
ad ann.
1221.
§.13,
gentlemen and hufoand men, Ecclefiafticall
& fecular flocked for to heare him, beholding
him as a man come from heauen, or an Angell
of the new teftament fent from God, to teach
heauenly things: inftructing the ignorant, con
uerting finners, and fetting vp a fchoole of
fanctity and perfection, his words were like
fire penetrating the hearts of his hearers, leauing them contrite and penitent, mollifying
the moft obdurate hearts; his preaching was

*The
fruites
of S. Fr.
preac-
hing.*
without humaine Rhetorike or Eloquence
but the holy Ghoft fpake by his mouth: many
amongft them ftaying with him to doe pennance, returned no more to their houfes;
others would haue forfaken wife and childrē,
houfes and liuings to follow him, and effect
his holy counfels; but the Saint Forbad them,
exhorting them to walke vprightly in the pre
fence of God, keeping his commandements
bringing vp their children and familie in the
feare of God shunning finne and vice: and
he would not faile to teach them the way to
heauen.

But all in vaine, for this people no longer
able to withftand the feruent impulfions of
the holy Ghoft, would not agree to re
turne vnto their houfes, vntill he had admit
ted and receiued them all for Brothers and

Sifters

Sisters of his Order, thus by diuine instinct the yeare 1221. the Seraphicall Father S. *Francis* instituted the third Order of pennance, which is for all sorts of persons, virgins, marryed, widdowes, both men and woemen, giuing them a Rule and forme of liuing, which might be obserued of all Christians liuing in the world, wherby they might amidst the stormes and surging seas of this life, offer vnto God their bodyes and soules as a pleasing and holy sacrifice. The Standardbearer, conductor, or eldest sonne of the third Order of Pennance, who first receiued the habit from S. *Francis*, was B. Lucius or Luchesius, who abandoning militarie employments, hauing bene a valiant Captaine, in the Guelphian faction, he now retired dedicating himselfe wholy to the seruice of God, visiting hospitalls, receiuing the poore into his house, practising all the works of mercy corporall, and spirituall: after his death he hath bene illustrious for many miracles.

This third Order of S. *Francis* in its beginning & first age, hath bene of so great esteeme, as generally all sorts of persons embraced this happy kind of life, many Archbishops, Bishops, and Ecclesiasticall Prelates of great authority, made it their whole ambition to be inrolled therin, together with many Emperours and Empresses, Kings, Queenes, Princes, and Princesses, with innumerable of lower ranck, many of them being Canonised or bea-

S. Bon.
c. 4. §. 5
Chro. p.
1. B. 9.
c. 1.
The in-
stitution
of the
Order
of pen-
nance.
Luc.
Wadd.
ad ann.
1221. §.
14.
Icem
1242 §.
7. 14.

L   tisyed

tifyed. For the satisfaction of the reader I will
here insert a Catologue of the most renowned
persons who haue made their entry into heauen, through this secure port S. Lewis the
pearle of kings most refulgent Sunne amongst
princes did illustrate that golden time *Henry*
king of Dacia, *S. Elzear* Cout of *Arian* of pro-
uence, S. *Iue* Priest wel versed in Ciuile & Ca-
non law, *B. Robert* Prince of *Riminie*, S. *Roth*
Sonne to a Prince liuing nere to *Mountpellier*,
B. Leo Archbishop of *Millan B. Chautter* Bishop
of *Tremise* illustrious for many miracles. *B.*
Bartholomew of *Geminiano* Priest who merited to
see *Iesus Christ* enuironed with a troope of Angells, *B. Conrade* of *Plaisance* beatifyed by *Leo*
the tenth

S. *Elizabeth* widdow daughter to the King
of *Hungarie*, S. *Iane* of the crosse, S. *Elizabeth*
queene of Portugall daughter to *Peter* King of
Arrogan, S. *Brigit* princesse of sweda, B. *Angela*
of Fulginia, B. *Iane* of Signa, B. *Margarit* of
Cortonne, B. *Rose* of *Viterbe*, B. *Viridian* B.
Clare of *Mont Falco* in whose heart after her
death was found imprinted a Crucifix with all
the mysteries of the passion of *Iesus Christ*. It
doth well appeare that our Lord speaking
to S. *Francis* by the *Crucifix*, did not say in
vaine *Goe Francis repaire my house which is*
ready to fall neither must wee vnderstand by
these words the restauration of the materiall
temples but the institution of the three Orders
signifyed by the three Churchs.

Of B. Hortulana *the* Mother *of* Sainte Clare.

CHAP. V.

THis noble Arke of Noe floting on the deluge repeopling the world, had but three lofts according to the saying of scripture, the incomparable Doctor saint Augustine allegorising hereon, sayth it was to signify the three estates in the Church; of virgins, widdowes, and marryed people: another Doctor discoursing hereupon compareth virginity to gold, widdowhood to siluer, & maryage to lead, as gold is the King of mettals and the most noble: euē so virginity is the most eminent & excelleth all other estates: Continency is compared to siluer for that it is an allay or matter more refined, and an estate more free: Maryage to lead, because it is a charge very burdensome and a heauy yoake Compassed with a thousand discontents, Iealousies, miseries, & misfortunes, so that many the first day of their marryage, haue not stuck to extoll the happy cōdition of those that were free because for one good day, they finde a hundred bad, and for one Rose of pleasure, a million of thornes of afflictions, others are impeached in the important busines of their saluation by the intrication of worldly affaires, which in

Gen.6.
S.Aug.
l.15.de
ciu.c.16
Theophil
in 1.Epi.
ad Tim.
4.

L 2   that

that state doth stop the progresse in spirituall life, hereof wee haue a liuely example in the Parable in the Ghospell where many being inuited to the Royall supper he only who had espoused a wife gaue the flat denyall, answering that his impediments were such, as he could not come.

Luc. 14

Neuertheles the condition is good, and needfull for the conseruation of the world, & pleasing to the diuine maiesty, for God himselfe hath bene the first author and institutor of it in the terrestriall Paradice, and state of Innocency, and hath ratified it with his presence, honouring it with his first miracles, at the wedding in Galile, it is a Sacrament which doth contribute grace, representing the vnion of the diuine word with humaine nature, of God with the soule, and of *Iesus Christ* with his Church: wherby many haue receiued singular and great fauours from our Lord, and haue in that estate bene adorned with rare perfections, and renowned in sacred histories. The B. *Hortulana* mother to the glorious virgin S. *Clare* was linked in matrimonie to a noble knight of the Citie of *Assisium* (called by the Italiens *Chise*) in the vaily of *Spoleto*: her husbands name was *Fauorin* Sonne to *Paule* of *Sassi* of an Illustrious Familie, hauing much wealth and riches, this Lady *Hortulana* bare vnto him three daughters by name *Clare Agnes*, and *Beatrix* they liued after a most honorable and eminent manner, holding the cheife ranke in the City both for

Gen. 2.

Ioan. 8.

Luc.
Wadd.
ad annū
1212, §.
14.
Petrus
Rodulp.
fol. 157.

                              thei

their noble extraction, exemplar life and virtuous acts, liuing in great peace and coniugall
affection , and admirable sympathie of hu-
mors: a thing most recommendable according
to the saying of the Wiseman , three things doe
infinitely content me and doe please both God
and man, peace between brethren, loue of our
neighbour and vnion betweene man and wife,
contrariwise to behold a marryed couple at
disagreement, is to see two enemies fastned to
one crosse, & two criminels chained together.
Hortulana exhibited honour and respect to her
husband as to her Lord, and Maister , confor-
ming her selfe to his will in all things iust and
lawfull; ruling her children and familie in the
feare of God ; and although she was busied
like S. *Martha* in her domesticall affaires
buying and prouiding things, necessarie in time
conuenient , hauing an eye to all things
for the gouuernment of her familie , being
not ignorant, that the care and vigilancie
of the Masters eye according to the Pro-
uerbe doth make Fat the horse and enrich
the ground. on the contrary she did not omit
to imbrace the condition of S. *Mary Magdalen*;
For she was very intense and feruent in
prayer, and most deuout in the enioying of
heauēly fauours; but aboue all shee felt vnspeakable sweetnes in the deuout contemplation
of the dolorous Passiō of our sacred Redeemer
Crsīt Iesus, from thence she drew inflamed desires to aduance her selfe in the loue of God,

L 3   she

she nourrished & releiued the poore, applying
her selfe to the works of mercy: This virtuous
Ladie did manifest the piety and great deuotiō
of her mind by many pilgrimages which she
vndertooke and pertormed both beyond & on
this side the seas: she visited with great feruour of spirit the tombes of the two Princes of
the Apostles S. *Peter* & S. *Paule* in the Citie of
Rome; she trauelled to the Church of the glorious Archangell S. *Michaell* on mount *Gorgonne*
in the kingdome of Naples, and which is more
with a manly courage and magnanimous spirit she passed the Seas with many other Pil
grimes and visited the holy Land and places
which our Redeemer *Christ Iesus* had confe-
crated with his sacred presence, from whence
she returned much consolated and enriched
with many merits: this custome truly was very
plaudable in our predecessors (but more admirable then imitable in the Feminine sex)
who with so great toyle, charges, incommodi-
ties and deuotion, haue performed this pietie
but is now so decayed, that the feruour a-
mongst Christians in visiting the places which
our Redeemer hath sanctisyed by his death and
Passion is almost quite extinguished by the
continuall warres betweene Christian Princes
(a thing most deplorable) in lieu that they
should bend all their forces and power against
the Enemies of God and the Catholike faith,
in imitation of the puissant Emperour and
King of France, S. *Charllemaigne* who deli-

uered

Chron. p
I *.l.* 8 *.c.*
I.
Luc.
Wadd.
ad annū
I2I2 §.
I3.

uered the Citie of *Hierusalem* and *Spaine* from
of the hard seruitude of the Saracens, of the
most Christian King of France *Lewis* who
tooke the strong Citie of *Damies* in *Egypt* and
wonne many notable victories ouer the enemies of God and Infidels: and by another long
iourney by sea he passed into Affricke with
a mighty nauy and strong Armie; but the
plague infected the whole Country wherof *Iohn* of France his sonne dyed with many
Earles and Barons of his Court, and finally he
himselfe was taken with it wherfore bowing
downe vnder the Palme before the Citie of
Thunes in *Affrick*, he there died. Of the valorous
& renowned *Godfrey* duke of Loraine who (for
this purpose sold his Dukedome of *Bullen* to
Albertus Bishop of *Liege*) and was chosen afterwards King of *Hierusalem*: of the most virtuous
Téterie of *Elsace* Count of Flanders : who trauelled foure times to the holy Land to recouer
certaine places forth of the possession of the
Turke and Barbarians, in requitall of these his
pious labours *Foulques* of *Ansoy* King of *Hieru-
sale* the year 1148 did giue vnto him some par-
cell of the sacred Bloud of our Redeemer
Christ Iesus gathered vp by *Ioseph* of *Aramathia*,
wherwith the Count inriched the Chap-
pell of S *Bassle* in the faire and magnificent Citie of *Bruges*: it is shewed to this very day euery fryday with great reuerence and deuotion;
it was brought from beyond sea by B. *Leo* Abbot of the most famous and renowned Abbey

*Saint
Lewys
Ribade-
neira in
his life.*

*Paule
emiss.
l.3.histor
Godfrey
Duke of
Bullen.*

*Peter
Onder-
gheest
Annal.
of Fland
c.737*

of)

of S, *Bartine*: finaly of the renowned *Baudrayne* Count of *Flanders* afterward created Empe rour of *Constantinople* for his noble exployts and martiall prowesse and trophies: leauing out of the list many other Christian Kings and Prin ces who haue exposed their kingdomes, riches and liues for to subdue and destroy the Barba rous nation of the *Sarrazins* and Turkes and set Free the holy Land which our Redeemer hath sanctifyed with his precious hloud and sacred presence.

The admirable patience of B. Hor-
tulana and how she became Re-
ligious and of her happy
death.

CHAP. VI.

THis virtuous Lady *Hortulana* perseue ring constant in the seruice of God ap plying her selfe to the exercises of true Christian pyetie, she merited to be prooued in the furnace of tribulation and affliction, the touchstone of true virtue and certainely many times our greatest happines is neer at hand knockig at the gate of our soule whe it is most replenished with sorrow and affliction, to this agreeth the saying of the Prophet *tribulation begets the knowledge of ones selfe, prosperity doth*

infatuate

infatuate and dull the spirit, and on the contrary affliction doth quicken the vnderstanding and produceth the knowledge of God & oneselfe: whē wee flow in delights wee forget heauē & neuer thinke of death; but when wee are on all sides assaulted with tribulatiōs, life becomes ireksome, wee long for death, all our thoughts desires and affections aspiring to heauen, the scourge of tribulation is for many respects very profitable to man, imbellishing the exteriour and interiour, doth compell the sinner perforce to turne vnto God, teacheth the ignorant, fortifyeth those that runne in the Race, defendeth the infirme, awaketh the sluggish, humbleth the proud and haughtie, purgeth the penitent, crowneth the innocent, augmenteth pietie and deuotion, and aduanceth the iust to all sanctity and perfection; as wee may find in many histories, but that of the B. *Hortulana* shall content vs for the present, she was linked with a most cordiall and inseparable loue to her husband *Fauorine* louing him as her owne soule and he conformable to his name, was most fauorable and endeeredly kind vnto her, now the Almighty Creatour to make tryall of his seruants patience and to draw her affection more intensiuely to himselfe: assaulted her on the part most sensible, depriuing her of her Husband by death incident to all the children of *Adam*: this seruant of Iesus Christ seeing her selfe thus depriued of her cheefest ioy and comfort, in the flower of her age, received this

M   affli-

affliction with inuincible patience, resounding
a most sweet harmonie in her suffrance saying
with the Prophet Iob *our Lord hath giuen, our
Lord hath taken, as it hath pleased our Lord so is it
done, the name of our Lord be blessed*, and with the
virtuous Ladie *Melanie* mentioned by *S. Hierome* who hauing lost her husband and two
children vpon one day casting her selfe on her
knees at the foot of the *Crucifix* sayd *I see
very well and plainly perceiue what it is that you
require of me my God, my loue and affection was
fastned vpon my husband and children you haue depriued me of them, desiring to possesse my loue alone
without any riuall. I willingly resigne it and consecrate it vnto you from my heart*: in like sort B.
Hortulana hauing lost her Husband by soudaine
and vnexpected death which makes the po-
tentates of the earth to stoope: with great
magnanimity vttered these words, *O my God and
soueraigne Creator, my loue was to fast setled vpon
my Husband wherfore you haue depriued me of him,
your holy name be praysed, now I doe wholy resigne and consecrate my soule and affection with all
I possesse in this world to your seruice*: but as great
exploits are not to be vndertaken and atchei-
ued without counsell and aduise, after that her
two daughters *Clare* and *Agnes* had forsaken the
world, hauing none left with her but her
litle *Beatrix*, she besought the holy Father S.
Francis to visit her and comfort her in her
widdowhood and afflictions, she discouered
and layd open vnto him the secrets of her

heart

heart, disclosing the desire she had to confecrate her selfe to God in the Conuent of her
daughter, forsaking all her Friends, riches,
and delights, the holy Father praysing and
magnifying God that he had the meanes to sacrifice both the Mother and the daughter to
his diuine Maiesty granted her suite, wherfore she following his wholesome aduise, dis-
posed of her house and familie, putting her
little daughter *Beatrix* into the custodie of a
noble knight called *Monaldo* brother to her
husband, destributing the remainder of her
goods most liberally to the poore, then the
Seraphicall Father cut of her haire at the Conuent of S. *Damian* giuing her the sacred veile
of Religion, and a course abiect habit of the
Order, (wherfore now to the honour of this
noble Ladie wee may sing with the Royall
Prophet *my soule blesse our Lord and all things
which are within me magnify his holy name*, who
hath filled me with good things, & accomplised the
desire of his seruant for her youth hath bene
renewed like vnto the Eagle, since that she
hauing attained to an elder age, did performe
the humble offices of Nouices and of young
Religious, with great feruour and allacrity of
spirit and being a Mother esteemed her selfe
happy to be the daughter to her daughter
yeelding her all Obedience, submission and reuerence vndergoing couragiously all the au-
sterities of the Order as fastings, watchings,
disciplines, and other such like mortifications,

*Pet. Ro-
dulph.
fol. 139.
Luc.
Wadd.
ad ann.
1253.
§. 25.
S. Fran-
cis giues
the habit
to B.
Hortula-
na.
Psal. 102*

Their virtues did combine them more strictly together in loue and affection, by how much more that grace and nature conioyned together is of more force then nature orly : this B. Hortulana was adorned with so great virtue and perfection that often times S. *Francis* and S. *Clare* did send vnto her many infirme afflicted creatures to be comforted and cured by her merits, and prayers: Ther was one day presented vnto S. *Clare* a child of Perusia hauing a Filme vpon his eye, she making the signe of the holy Crosse vpon the eye, sent the child to Sister Hortulana who also blessed it, and the child was presently cured, whervpon there arose a holy debate amongst the Religious whether this miracle proceeded from the merits of the daughter, or the Mother, but S. *Clare* ended the striffe assuring them that Sister Hortulana was of power to doe great matters with the diuine Maiesty, finally this good Lady imbellished with many rare virtues and perfections left this transitorie life to enioy the eternall in the vision and fruition of God who hath adorned her with the splendor of miracles before and after her death, she was buried at S. *Damians*, and after translated to the Church of S. *George* where she is now intombed with her two davghters S. *Clare* and B. *Agnes*.

Chr. p. I
l. 8 c, 21
Wadd.

The death of B Hortulana.

Of